Marketing

Operations

Finance

Human Resource Management

Answers to Quick Tests

Preparing to learn

About this Success Guide

This book has been written to help you succeed in your Intermediate 1 (Int 1) or Intermediate 2 (Int 2) Business Management course. It has been written so that you can learn about each of the main topics in your course, to help you with your class work and assessments. There is also a section for you to **track your learning** when preparing for your assessments.

Each section in this book starts off with the basics about a topic and is contained within **blue** boxes; you need to know all of this information for Int 1 and for Int 2. If you need to know more for Int 2, this will come after the basics and is contained within **green** boxes.

As you go through each section in this book, you will see different features being used. On each spread you will see **Top Tips, Key Concepts** and **Quick Tests**.

Top Tips – these boxes have very useful advice for you so that you can do the best you can in your assessments and exams. You should think carefully about the advice given in these boxes because it will help you to avoid making mistakes in exams!

Key Concepts – these boxes help you to understand the main point of a topic.

Quick Tests – these come at the end of each section. You can find the answers to the questions at the back of this book. If you are studying for Int 2 you should attempt both the Int 1 and Int 2 questions!

Top Tip
If you are studying Int 1, learn the information within the blue boxes only. If you are studying Int 2, learn the information from within the blue **and** green boxes.

Your course

Your course is made up of three units and an exam. To pass the course, you need to pass each of the three units and the exam. *(More information on assessment is provided later.)* The main topics within each course are almost the same, but the names given to the units are different, depending on which level you are studying.

Intermediate 1 Business Management	Intermediate 2 Business Management
The three units are:	The three units are:
Unit 1 – Business Enterprise	**Unit 1** – Business Enterprise
Unit 2 – Business Decision Areas	**Unit 2** – Business Decision Areas: Marketing and Operations
Unit 3 – Business Information and ICT	**Unit 3** – Business Decision Areas: Finance and Human Resource Management

Assessment

As well as tests your teacher may have done with you in class, you have to complete formal and very important pieces of assessment that demonstrate what you have learned. There is one assessment for each of the three units: these assessments are known as NABs. Each NAB is one hour long and is marked by your teacher. To pass a NAB, you need to earn at least half of the available marks; if you don't pass the first time round, you will usually be given another chance to show what you have learned. You must pass the three NABs to be able

Key Concepts

A NAB is an assessment (a test) that will show if you have learned enough to pass a unit.

to sit the exam at the end of the course and (provided you pass the exam), achieve the award of Intermediate 1 or Intermediate 2 Business Management.

At the very end of your course, you will sit an exam that has been put together by the Scottish Qualifications Authority (SQA). This exam has been written by a small team of very experienced teachers for the SQA and only this team knows what the questions in the exam will be. Your teacher will not know until after you have sat your exam what questions will come up!

You need to make sure you are prepared for this exam so that you can do as well as you possibly can. If you pass this exam, you will receive a certificate showing what grade you have achieved – A, B or C.

The Int 1 exam	The exam lasts for 1 hour and 15 minutes and is split into two sections. Both sections have a small case study you are required to read and then answer questions on. Each section is worth 25 marks, making 50 marks available for the whole exam.
The Int 2 exam	The exam lasts for 1 hour and 45 minutes and is split into two sections. Section 1 is based on a case-study that you are required to read and answer questions on. Section 2 contains five questions and you are required to choose and answer any two of these. Section 1 is worth 25 marks and each question in Section 2 is worth 25 marks, making 75 marks available for the whole exam paper.

Further information about your exam can be found on the next page.

Exam technique

Introduction

Doing well in any assessment or exam comes down to two things: (1) how much you have learned and (2) how good your exam technique is. You might have lots of knowledge in your head, but you need to know how to show the person marking your exam paper that you have read the question and written down what has been asked for. By reading this section of this book you should be able to improve your exam technique and hopefully gain extra marks! (And extra marks will hopefully mean a better grade!)

Top Tip

Good exam technique is crucial to doing well in your exam.

How do I learn?

Everybody learns in different ways and you need to find out how you learn best. Some people need to have a quiet environment to learn in and some people learn better while listening to music. **You need to find out the way you learn best**.

You need to get yourself organised with plenty of pens, paper and a notebook or folder so that you can organise your notes. You might decide that you want to work through this book and then try some past paper questions. Remember that everyone is different – you need to find a way that works for you.

You also need to think about how to organise yourself to help you in your revision; you might find it useful to create a revision timetable that shows you what you will be revising for each subject and when. **Revision for your exam is very important!**

A revision timetable might look like this:

	6pm – 6:50pm	7pm – 7:50pm	8pm – 9pm
Monday	Business Mgt	Maths	Homework
Tuesday	Homework	Admin	Chemistry
Wednesday	Music	Business Mgt	Maths
Thursday	Free	Homework	History
Friday	Free	Free	Free
Saturday	Homework	English	Business Mgt
Sunday	History	Admin	Music

You can never do too much revision, but you need to make sure that you give your brain a rest and take regular breaks. Your brain also likes plenty of water (not fizzy drinks!) and fresh air so make sure you get these too.

The exam paper

The Int 1 paper is printed on **blue** paper and the Int 2 paper is printed on **green** paper. At Int 1, you write your answers on the exam paper but at Int 2 you are given a separate answer booklet. Before reading any of the questions in the exam you should:

- Check that you have been given the correct exam paper.
- Read the instructions on the front of the exam paper carefully. (Make sure you know how much time you have, how many questions you need to answer and where to write down your answers.)
- Ensure you have a separate answer booklet if you are sitting Int 2.
- Fill in the front cover of your exam paper (or answer booklet) with your name, candidate number and details about your school or college carefully and neatly.

Questions and command words

Your exam will contain questions for you to answer. The questions are based on what you have been taught during the course and will assess all three units that you studied. Each question in your exam paper is very carefully put together: each will have a **command word** that gives you an instruction on what to do.

Top Tip
You must make sure you know what each command word means so that you can correctly answer each question.

Key Concepts

Command words are very important; they are instructions on how to answer questions. You must pay attention to the command word(s) within a question or you will not answer it correctly.

If you ignore the command word, there is a good chance that you will not answer the question correctly. It is a good idea to underline or highlight the command word (or words) in each question before you begin to answer it.

Intermediate 1 command words	
Define	State the exact meaning of the word or phrase
Describe	Give a full account of the word, phrase etc
Give	Pick some key factors and name them
Identify	Name the main point or points
List	State the main factors (with no explanation or elaboration)
Name	Identify or make a list
Outline	Give the main features
State	Present in a brief form
Suggest	State a possible reason or course of action (no development required)

Intermediate 2 command words	
Compare	Identify similarities and differences between two or more factors
Define	Give a clear meaning of the word or phrase
Describe	Provide a thorough description of something
Distinguish	Identify the differences between two or more factors
Explain	Give details about how and why something is as it is. You must make sure you give a reason for something being a benefit or consequence. (To get a mark for an 'explain' question, your answer will need to have two parts.)
Give	Pick some key factors and name them
Identify	Give the name or identifying characteristics of something
Name	Identify or make a list
Outline	State the main features
Suggest	State a possible reason or course of action (no development required)

You should get lots of practice in answering exam questions before your exam. You can download past papers free of charge from the SQA's website and your teacher may mark some of these for you.

You should look at the mark available for each question and use this as a guide to the length of answer you require. It is very important that you manage your time carefully in the exam so that you have time to answer all of the questions that you have to.

This book will also help you develop your exam technique. Many of the questions are worded similarly to those in NABs and in exams. You should make sure you look at each one and the command word carefully when answering it. For those studying Int 2, there is advice on how to tackle different command words and also plenty of examples of how to answer 'explain' questions successfully.

Top Tip
You need to read the instructions throughout the exam paper very carefully. Don't throw marks away by not reading the question carefully!

Golden Rules for Exams!

- Find out which way you learn best.
- Revise, revise, revise! (But make sure to take breaks too.)
- Keep your revision notes organised.
- Read the exam instructions and questions carefully.
- Write neatly on the exam paper.
- Practice as many past exam paper questions as you can.
- Make sure you know what the command words mean.
- Get a good night's sleep before each exam.
- Sit the exam knowing you have revised hard and are trying your best – no matter what grade you get.

Track your learning (Intermediate 1)

Now that you know how the course is structured and will be assessed, you can get on with learning! This section will enable you to **check your progress** and **record any areas that are causing you concern**. It has been designed for you to use when preparing for your NABs, preliminary examination and SQA examination.

Listed below are the different topic areas as defined by the SQA. When your NABs, preliminary examination and SQA examination are approaching, you should rate yourself on how confident you are on each topic. You should base what you know on evidence, for example feedback from your teacher, results of homework exercises and from attempting past paper questions on that particular topic.

The rating system given is based on a set of traffic lights: **green** means you understand the topic fully, amber means you have an understanding of the main points but there are gaps in your knowledge and **red** means you have only a little or no knowledge of that topic. Where you are unsure of something, the page numbers you should refer to in this guide are given so you know exactly where to look for the information. **There are no excuses for not knowing something**!

UNIT 1	Knowledge for NAB	Knowledge for prelim	Knowledge for SQA exam	Page number
Business, needs and wants				14
Goods and services				14
Creating wealth				15
Sectors of business activity				15
What is enterprise?				16
Factors of production				16
Types of business				18–20
Objectives				22
Stakeholders				24
Sources of finance				26
What influences business?				28
Why grow?				30
NAB RESULT _____/25 DATE_____				

UNIT 2	Knowledge for NAB	Knowledge for prelim	Knowledge for SQA exam	Page number
What is marketing?				54
The marketing mix – the 4 'P's				56
Product life cycle				58
What is a brand?				60
Market segments				60
Pricing strategies				62
Place				64

	Knowledge for NAB	Knowledge for prelim	Knowledge for SQA exam	Page number
Promotion and advertising	▣ ▣ ▣	▣ ▣ ▣	▣ ▣ ▣	66
Market research	▣ ▣ ▣	▣ ▣ ▣	▣ ▣ ▣	68
What is Operations?	▣ ▣ ▣	▣ ▣ ▣	▣ ▣ ▣	72
Choosing a supplier	▣ ▣ ▣	▣ ▣ ▣	▣ ▣ ▣	73
Stock control	▣ ▣ ▣	▣ ▣ ▣	▣ ▣ ▣	74
Job, batch and flow production	▣ ▣ ▣	▣ ▣ ▣	▣ ▣ ▣	76–77
Managing quality	▣ ▣ ▣	▣ ▣ ▣	▣ ▣ ▣	80
Role of Finance	▣ ▣ ▣	▣ ▣ ▣	▣ ▣ ▣	82
Financial information	▣ ▣ ▣	▣ ▣ ▣	▣ ▣ ▣	84–85
Cash flow	▣ ▣ ▣	▣ ▣ ▣	▣ ▣ ▣	86–87
What is HRM?	▣ ▣ ▣	▣ ▣ ▣	▣ ▣ ▣	92
Stages in recruitment	▣ ▣ ▣	▣ ▣ ▣	▣ ▣ ▣	94–95
Stages in selection	▣ ▣ ▣	▣ ▣ ▣	▣ ▣ ▣	98
Types of training	▣ ▣ ▣	▣ ▣ ▣	▣ ▣ ▣	102
Appraisals	▣ ▣ ▣	▣ ▣ ▣	▣ ▣ ▣	102
Payment methods	▣ ▣ ▣	▣ ▣ ▣	▣ ▣ ▣	104
Employee relations	▣ ▣ ▣	▣ ▣ ▣	▣ ▣ ▣	104
Law and the workplace	▣ ▣ ▣	▣ ▣ ▣	▣ ▣ ▣	106

NAB RESULT _____ /25   **DATE**_____

UNIT 3	Knowledge for NAB	Knowledge for prelim	Knowledge for SQA exam	Page number
Sources of information	▣ ▣ ▣	▣ ▣ ▣	▣ ▣ ▣	32
Types of information	▣ ▣ ▣	▣ ▣ ▣	▣ ▣ ▣	32
Uses of information	▣ ▣ ▣	▣ ▣ ▣	▣ ▣ ▣	36
ICT in business	▣ ▣ ▣	▣ ▣ ▣	▣ ▣ ▣	38
Hardware	▣ ▣ ▣	▣ ▣ ▣	▣ ▣ ▣	38
Software	▣ ▣ ▣	▣ ▣ ▣	▣ ▣ ▣	39
The internet	▣ ▣ ▣	▣ ▣ ▣	▣ ▣ ▣	40
Other types of ICT	▣ ▣ ▣	▣ ▣ ▣	▣ ▣ ▣	41–43

NAB RESULT _____ /25   **DATE**_____

Preliminary examination result   Mark _____% Grade _____   Date _____

Once you have done your preliminary examination and have your result, you will be in a good position to make a list of actions you need to take to help improve your final examination result. You should record these in the table below.

Action number	What action do I need to take to improve my final result?	Date completed and notes
1		
2		
3		

Please do not underestimate the effort and work you need to put in to do well.

Remember – there is only one mark's difference between getting an A or a B, and between a C and a fail. One mark makes all the difference! The more work you put in, the greater the chance of getting a higher grade.

Track your learning (Intermediate 2)

Now that you know how the course is structured and will be assessed, you can get on with learning! This section will enable you to **check your progress** and **record any areas that are causing you concern**. It has been designed for you to use when preparing for your NABs, preliminary examination and SQA examination.

Listed below are the different topic areas as defined by the SQA. When your NABs, preliminary examination and SQA examination are approaching, you should rate yourself on how confident you are on each topic. You should base what you know on evidence, for example the feedback you have from your teacher, results of homework exercises and attempting past paper questions on that particular topic.

The rating system given is based on a set of traffic lights: **green** means you understand the topic fully, **amber** means you have an understanding of the main points but there are gaps in your knowledge and **red** means you have only a little or no knowledge of that topic. Where you are unsure of something, the page numbers you should refer to in this guide are given so you know exactly where to look for the information. **There are no excuses for not knowing something**!

UNIT 1	Knowledge for NAB	Knowledge for prelim	Knowledge for SQA exam	Page number
Enterprise and entrepreneurs	■ ■ ■	■ ■ ■	■ ■ ■	16–17
Factors of production	■ ■ ■	■ ■ ■	■ ■ ■	17
Types of businesses	■ ■ ■	■ ■ ■	■ ■ ■	18–21
Objectives	■ ■ ■	■ ■ ■	■ ■ ■	22–23
Stakeholders	■ ■ ■	■ ■ ■	■ ■ ■	24–25
Sources of finance	■ ■ ■	■ ■ ■	■ ■ ■	26–27
Changes in business	■ ■ ■	■ ■ ■	■ ■ ■	28–29
Growth	■ ■ ■	■ ■ ■	■ ■ ■	30–31
Sources and types of information	■ ■ ■	■ ■ ■	■ ■ ■	32–35
Hardware and software	■ ■ ■	■ ■ ■	■ ■ ■	38–39
The internet	■ ■ ■	■ ■ ■	■ ■ ■	40
Other types of ICT	■ ■ ■	■ ■ ■	■ ■ ■	41–43
Costs and benefits of ICT	■ ■ ■	■ ■ ■	■ ■ ■	43
Management roles	Internal organisation does not appear in the NAB	■ ■ ■	■ ■ ■	44
Types of decision		■ ■ ■	■ ■ ■	45
Decision-making model		■ ■ ■	■ ■ ■	46–47
Organisations and structures		■ ■ ■	■ ■ ■	48–53

NAB RESULT _____ /40   DATE_____

UNIT 2

Role of marketing	Knowledge for NAB	Knowledge for prelim	Knowledge for SQA exam	Page number
Role of marketing	☐ ☐ ☐	☐ ☐ ☐	☐ ☐ ☐	54–55
The marketing mix – the 4 'P's	☐ ☐ ☐	☐ ☐ ☐	☐ ☐ ☐	56–57
Product life cycle	☐ ☐ ☐	☐ ☐ ☐	☐ ☐ ☐	58–59
Branding	☐ ☐ ☐	☐ ☐ ☐	☐ ☐ ☐	60
Market segments	☐ ☐ ☐	☐ ☐ ☐	☐ ☐ ☐	60–61
Pricing strategies	☐ ☐ ☐	☐ ☐ ☐	☐ ☐ ☐	62–63
Channels of distribution	☐ ☐ ☐	☐ ☐ ☐	☐ ☐ ☐	64–65
Promotion	☐ ☐ ☐	☐ ☐ ☐	☐ ☐ ☐	66–67
Market research	☐ ☐ ☐	☐ ☐ ☐	☐ ☐ ☐	68–71
Role and elements of Operations	☐ ☐ ☐	☐ ☐ ☐	☐ ☐ ☐	72–73
Purchasing and stock management	☐ ☐ ☐	☐ ☐ ☐	☐ ☐ ☐	74–75
Types of production	☐ ☐ ☐	☐ ☐ ☐	☐ ☐ ☐	76–79
Managing quality	☐ ☐ ☐	☐ ☐ ☐	☐ ☐ ☐	80–81

NAB RESULT _____ /40   DATE_____

UNIT 3

Role of Finance	Knowledge for NAB	Knowledge for prelim	Knowledge for SQA exam	Page number
Role of Finance	☐ ☐ ☐	☐ ☐ ☐	☐ ☐ ☐	82
Uses of financial information	☐ ☐ ☐	☐ ☐ ☐	☐ ☐ ☐	83
Trading, profit and loss	☐ ☐ ☐	☐ ☐ ☐	☐ ☐ ☐	84
Balance sheet	☐ ☐ ☐	☐ ☐ ☐	☐ ☐ ☐	85
Cash flow and budgets	☐ ☐ ☐	☐ ☐ ☐	☐ ☐ ☐	86–87
Users of financial information	☐ ☐ ☐	☐ ☐ ☐	☐ ☐ ☐	88
Ratio analysis	☐ ☐ ☐	☐ ☐ ☐	☐ ☐ ☐	90–91
HRM and working practices	☐ ☐ ☐	☐ ☐ ☐	☐ ☐ ☐	92–93
Recruitment	☐ ☐ ☐	☐ ☐ ☐	☐ ☐ ☐	94–97
Selection	☐ ☐ ☐	☐ ☐ ☐	☐ ☐ ☐	98–101
Types of training	☐ ☐ ☐	☐ ☐ ☐	☐ ☐ ☐	102
Appraisals	☐ ☐ ☐	☐ ☐ ☐	☐ ☐ ☐	102–103
Payment methods	☐ ☐ ☐	☐ ☐ ☐	☐ ☐ ☐	104
Methods of industrial action	☐ ☐ ☐	☐ ☐ ☐	☐ ☐ ☐	105
Contracts of employment	☐ ☐ ☐	☐ ☐ ☐	☐ ☐ ☐	105
Law and the workplace	☐ ☐ ☐	☐ ☐ ☐	☐ ☐ ☐	106–107

NAB RESULT _____ /40   DATE_____

Preliminary examination result   Mark _____% Grade _____   Date _____

Once you have done your preliminary examination and have your result, you will be in a good position to make a list of actions you need to take to help improve your final examination result. You should record these in the table below.

Action number	What action do I need to take to improve my final result?	Date completed and notes
1		
2		
3		

Please do not underestimate the effort and work you need to put in to do well.

Remember – there is only one mark's difference between getting an A or a B, and between a C and a fail. One mark makes all the difference! The more work you put in, the greater the chance of getting a higher grade.

What is business?

Business, needs and wants

TRAVEL AGENT

We might not realise it, but we all come into contact with businesses every day; we might buy something from a shop, visit the dentist or use a mobile phone and, without business, we wouldn't be able to do any of these things.

Remember, Int 1 material is in **blue** boxes.

Int 2 students need to read the **blue** boxes **and** the **green** boxes.

Businesses provide us with things that we use in our daily lives.

Some of these things are essential to life. These are known as **needs**. Examples include food, water, clothing and shelter. We also have **wants**, which are the extra things that we like to have to make our lives better, for example, mobile phones, computer games and holidays. The important difference between needs and wants is that needs are essential for survival, whereas wants are not.

Key Concepts

Needs are essential for us to be able to live (for example, food, clothing) whereas **wants** are extra things that we like to have (for example, mobile phones, computer games).

Goods and services

Businesses *produce* **goods** and **services** to help satisfy our needs and wants and we *consume* these goods and services by using them up.

Businesses spend lots of money and time on research and planning, to encourage us to buy their goods and services and to find ways of improving them.

The diagram below shows the difference between goods and services and also the difference between different types of goods (durable and non-durable).

Top Tip
You should practise writing down the definition of goods and services and give examples of each.

What is the difference between goods and services?

Goods
We can see, touch and feel these, for example, sweets, cans of juice, computer games, jars of coffee, books.

Durable
Can be used again and again until they break or wear out, for example, cars, computers, washing machines.

Non-durable
Can only be used once, for example, food, juice, flowers.

Services
These are provided for us, and we cannot touch or see them. They are provided by, for example, dentist, hairdresser, hotel, bank, restaurant, transport providers (for example, bus, train, air).

Creating wealth

Businesses create wealth for themselves by adding value to the products they make.

Katie has her own business making fruit cereal bars.

Before Katie can sell her fruit cereal bars to her customers, she has to make them.
She does this by going through the following steps.

Adding Value

1. She buys the necessary ingredients. (This costs her 20p per cereal bar.)
2. She puts the ingredients into a bowl and mixes them.
3. She then puts her mixed ingredients into a tray to set.
4. Once set, she takes the one large cereal bar out of the tray.
5. She cuts the one large bar into smaller bars.
6. The smaller bars are put into wrappers, ready to be sold for 50p each.

As Katie goes through each stage, **value is being added** to the price of the product.

When Katie finally sells her cereal bars to customers for 50p each, she will have made 30p profit on each bar. This is how a business makes money and creates wealth.

Sectors of business activity

Top Tip
Use examples in your answers when you can.

So far we have learned that businesses produce goods and services to satisfy the needs and wants of their customers. By doing so, they create wealth by adding value to the price of the goods or services they provide. Businesses belong to sectors of business activity, depending on what they do.

Primary sector	Businesses that belong to this sector take raw materials (basic materials needed to make something else) from the ground or sea. For example, fishing and farming
Secondary sector	Businesses that belong to this sector take raw materials and use these to make something else. For example, food manufacturers, builders and car manufacturers
Tertiary sector	Businesses that belong to this sector provide a service. For example, supermarkets/shops, schools, hairdressers and dentists

Quick Test I

Intermediate 1

1. State the difference between a need and a want.
2. Give an example of a need.
3. Give an example of a want.
4. Give two examples of a business that offers a service.
5. Define the term 'creating wealth'.
6. Describe what is meant by the primary sector.
7. Give two examples of a business that belongs to the tertiary sector.

Top Tip
See page 8 for definitions of command words.

Enterprise and entrepreneurs

What is enterprise?

There are lots of examples of famous entrepreneurs including Richard Branson (Virgin Group), Bill Gates (Microsoft), Anita Roddick (The Body Shop) and James Dyson (Dyson).

> **Key Concepts**
>
> **Enterprise** is being able to think of a business idea and developing it to make it successful; this is often done by someone known as an **entrepreneur**.

To become a successful entrepreneur is not as easy as you might think. You need to have several skills and qualities and to be willing to work hard, take risks and make decisions.

Barry has a business idea and wants to start his own business.

He needs to have different skills and qualities to turn his business idea into a successful business.

- Hardworking
- Confident
- Determined
- Computer skills
- People skills
- Creative
- Problem-solving skills
- Enthusiastic
- Financial skills
- Decision-making skills
- Risk-taker
- Motivated
- Sales skills
- Independent
- Organised
- Leadership skills
- Enterprising

The entrepreneur has a role to play and has to:

- think of a business idea by looking at what already exists and then trying to find something new that people would want
- bring together and combine different resources (factors of production: land, labour, capital and enterprise) to produce a product
- make decisions (for example, what product to make, what price to charge and what staff to employ)
- take risks to turn the idea into a success. Examples of risks an entrepreneur might take include: losing the money invested in the business or finding out that nobody wants to buy the product, in other words, that there is no *demand* for it.

> **Key Concepts**
>
> The **factors of production** (land, labour, capital and enterprise) are the different resources that entrepreneurs combine to turn their ideas into reality.

Risk-taking

Entrepreneurs have to take risks to turn their business ideas into successes. A risk is taken when someone tries something but isn't sure what might happen. For example, you run the risk of failing your Business Management course if you don't revise!

Entrepreneurs run the risk of losing their own money (their investment) if their businesses are not successful. They also run the risk of people not wanting to buy the goods or services they have developed and therefore their businesses could fail.

Factors of production

The factors of production (land, labour, capital and enterprise) are the different resources the entrepreneur combines to turn an idea into a reality.

Land	The natural resources of the world, for example, fields, trees, water, sunshine
Labour	The human effort (the workforce) required to make a product
Capital	The machinery, tools and equipment used to make a product and the money (financial investment) used to start the business
Enterprise	The entrepreneur combines all of the factors of production

Explaining the role of the entrepreneur

At Int 2, you might be asked to **explain** the role of the entrepreneur. At Int 1, you won't be asked to do this: you would only be asked to **describe** the role of the entrepreneur.

When answering an explain question, you have to give a reason for the idea/ suggestion you make. In other words, give a reason **why**.

Let's compare the difference between **describing** the role of the entrepreneur and **explaining** it. What you need to add to your answer so that you have explained it is highlighted in red in the table below.

Top Tip
It is very important that you know the difference between answering a **describe** question and an **explain** question.

At Intermediate 1 you might be asked to *Describe the role of the entrepreneur.*	At Intermediate 2 you might be asked to *Explain the role of the entrepreneur.*
• Thinks of a new business idea by looking at which goods or services already exist	• Thinks of a new business idea by looking at what already exists so that he or she produces a good or service that is more likely to be successful and profitable as it doesn't already exist.
• Brings together and combines the four factors of production	• Brings together and combines the four factors of production in the most efficient and cost-effective way by ensuring that the best use of each one is being achieved.
• Makes different decisions (for example, what product to make, what price to charge and what staff to employ)	• Makes different decisions (for example, what product to make, what price to charge and what staff to employ) with the intention of making the best decisions in the best interests of the success of the business.

Quick Test 2

Intermediate 1

1. Name the four factors of production.
2. Describe the term 'entrepreneur'.
3. Give an example of an entrepreneur.
4. Describe the role of the entrepreneur.
5. Suggest two risks (or problems) that an entrepreneur faces.

Intermediate 2

1. Describe the four factors of production.
2. Explain the role of the entrepreneur.

Types of business organisation

Private sector organisations

The main aim of organisations in the private sector is to make profit.

The four main types of businesses that belong to the private sector are:

- Sole Traders
- Partnerships
- Private Limited Companies
- Public Limited Companies

Top Tip
Make a note for each type of business: what it is, who owns it, who runs it, two advantages and two disadvantages.

	Sole Trader	Partnership
What is it?	A business owned by one person	A business owned by 2 to 20 people
Who is the owner?	The sole trader	The partners
Who runs it on a daily basis?	The sole trader	The partners
Where does the start-up finance (capital) come from?	The sole trader	The partners
Two advantages	• Easy to set up • Owner gets to keep the profits	• Workload and responsibility can be shared • More different ideas available compared to a sole trader
Two disadvantages	• Nobody to share workload and responsibility with • Difficult to get large amounts of finance (capital)	• Arguments between partners might happen • Profits have to be split between partners
Examples	Small businesses are usually sole traders, for example, newsagents or plumbers. An example could be Brian Smith Plumbing.	Small or medium-sized businesses are usually partnerships, for example, doctors or accountants. An example could be Adams and McNeill Accountants.

A **limited company** is different from a sole trader or partnership, because to be an owner of a limited company you need to buy shares in that company.

There are two types of limited company: **Private Limited Company** (Ltd) and **Public Limited Company** (Plc).

	Private Limited Company	Public Limited Company
What is it?	A company that is owned by shareholders. These are people who have bought shares in the company. Shares in a private limited company are usually sold to family or friends.	A company that is owned by shareholders. These are people who have bought shares in the company. Shares in a public limited company are available for anybody to buy from the stock market.
Who is the owner?	The shareholders	The shareholders
Who runs it on a daily basis?	The board of directors and managers	The board of directors and managers

Where does the start-up finance (capital) come from?	From the sale of shares privately to family and/or friends	From the sale of shares to anyone on the stock market
Two advantages	• Limited liability • Risk and responsibility are shared	• Limited liability • Large amounts of finance can be raised by selling more shares
Two disadvantages	• More difficult to set up than a sole trader or partnership • Company has to follow the rules laid down by the Companies Act	• Company has to publish its financial accounts every year • There is no control over who can buy shares
Examples	Private limited companies have Ltd after their name. Examples include Rena Craig Travel Ltd and Evelyn Kelly Beauty Ltd.	Public limited companies have Plc after their name. Many banks are Plcs. Examples include Gillies Financial Services Plc and The Royal Bank of Scotland Plc.

Key Concepts

Limited liability means that if the company goes bankrupt, shareholders only lose the money they have spent purchasing their shares. They will not lose their own personal belongings (for example, their cars or houses). The opposite is **unlimited liability** which sole traders and partnerships have.

Public sector (publicly funded) organisations

The main aim of organisations in the public sector is to provide services.

These organisations are owned by the government. They are also run and managed by the government.

Public sector (**publicly-funded**) organisations are funded through taxes. People have to pay tax on a number of things including the wages they earn and items that they buy. These taxes are then used to provide services throughout the country.

Examples of publicly-funded organisations include the NHS, schools, local councils, the police and the BBC.

Top Tip
Do not confuse **public limited companies** with **public sector organisations**. They are different!

Voluntary sector organisations

The main aim of organisations in the voluntary sector is to help specific causes.

Charities are a common example of an organisation in the voluntary sector. Charities are overseen (regulated) by the government but they are run by boards of trustees. Many people who work for charities are volunteers, that is to say they receive no money for the work that they do.

Charities exist to help many different causes. For example:

• The SSPCA aims to help prevent animals from suffering
• Save the Children aims to provide education, healthcare and food to suffering children
• Age UK aims to improve the quality of life for older people.

Top Tip
Organisations in the public and voluntary sectors **do not** aim to make a profit.

Quick Test 3

Intermediate 1

1. Identify what the letters Ltd stand for.
2. Identify what the letters Plc stand for.
3. Describe what is meant by a sole trader.
4. Give an advantage of being a sole trader.
5. Describe what is meant by a partnership.
6. Give an advantage of being in a partnership.
7. Describe what is meant by a public sector organisation.
8. Name a type of organisation that belongs to the voluntary sector.

Types of organisation at Intermediate 2

It is important at Int 2 that you know a bit more detail than is required at Int 1. The purpose of the following section is to provide you with more detail about different types of business organisations. **You should read this section after you have read and completed the Int 1 section on types of business organisations.**

Private sector organisations

Sole traders (or self-employed people) usually have small businesses and do not usually operate around the country or all over the world. Sometimes a sole trader might employ other people to help with the work. Other advantages and disadvantages include:

Advantages	Disadvantages
• Owner can choose which hours to work. • Owner gets to make all the decisions.	• Owner has no-one to share responsibility, workload or problems with. • There is unlimited liability for the owner.

Partnerships are also usually small or medium-sized businesses. They might operate locally or all over the country. Partnerships may have other staff working for them. Other advantages and disadvantages include:

Advantages	Disadvantages
• Each partner often brings different experiences and skills. • Partnerships find it easier to obtain finance than sole traders. • Risks and decision-making are shared.	• Partners have unlimited liability. • A legal agreement between partners needs to be set up detailing how profits will be split.

When a company is being set up (a Ltd or a Plc), two documents have to be created: a **memorandum of association** and **articles of association**. These are sent to Companies House which keeps a register of all companies that have been set up. Both kinds of companies have, in addition to a board of directors, staff who are employed to work for them.

Private limited companies (Ltds) are owned by a minimum of one shareholder and run by a board of directors which has been appointed by shareholders. By law, there must be at least one director and a company secretary. Quite often Ltds are businesses whose shares are owned by different family members. Other advantages and disadvantages include:

Top Tip
You need to be able to describe different types of organisation in terms of who owns it, who controls it, how it is financed and advantages and disadvantages.

Advantages	Disadvantages
• Experience and skills from shareholders and directors • More sources of finance available than a sole trader or partnership	• Annual company accounts are available publicly • There are often high start-up costs

Public limited companies (Plcs) must have at least two shareholders. Other advantages and disadvantages include:

Advantages	Disadvantages
• More sources of finance available than for a sole trader or partnership • Because of their size, can take advantage of economies of scale (for example, discounts on buying large amounts of raw materials)	• Company has to adhere to the rules and regulations of the Companies Act

At Int 2 you also need to know about **franchises**. This is where a business person provides a product or service supplied by another business. More information on franchises is given on page 31.

Explaining advantages and disadvantages

The advantages and disadvantages of each type of business organisation given in this book have already been **described**. However, you might be asked to **explain** them. This means you have to give a reason why something is an advantage or a disadvantage. Let's explain the advantages and disadvantages of a sole trader as an example. What you need to add to your answer to ensure that you have explained it is highlighted in red in the table below.

Sole trader – advantages explained	Sole trader – disadvantages explained
• Easy to set up which means that it can be started, and generate income, quickly. • Owner gets to keep the profits and therefore does not have to split these with other people. • Owner can decide which hours to work and can choose when to start and finish, meaning they can work whenever it suits them, giving them a better work/life balance. • Owner gets to make all the decisions and therefore decisions can be made more quickly.	• Nobody to share workload and responsibility with which could be stressful for the owner. • Difficult to get large amounts of finance (capital) which could be a problem if the owner wants the business to expand. • Owner has no-one to share responsibility, workload or problems with and this could cause problems if he or she wants to take time off, for example, for a holiday. • Unlimited liability for the owner which means they have the risk of losing their own personal assets (for example, car) if the business fails.

Objectives

What are objectives?

 An objective (or aim) is a goal or target for a business to work towards. It is something for the business to achieve in the future and helps decide what action should be taken to move the company forward.

An objective of a business might be to **make a profit**. To achieve this objective, the business must decide what action to take to achieve this.

Different types of business might have similar and different objectives.

Objectives of private sector organisations

The main objective of private sector organisations is to **make profit**. However, they have other objectives including:

- to survive
- to grow
- to offer quality goods or services
- to have a strong brand identity
- to be the market leader.

Objectives of public sector organisation

The main objective of a public sector (publicly funded) organisation is to **provide a service**. However, they have other objectives including:

- to meet the needs of local people
- to stick to an agreed budget
- to have a good image.

Objectives of voluntary organisations

The main objective of a voluntary organisation is to **help a particular cause**. The particular cause will depend on the exact charity. However, they have other objectives including:

- to spend donations in the best way possible
- to promote the cause/charity
- to increase the number of volunteers
- to increase donations.

Describing objectives

At Int 2, you will also be asked to identify different objectives for different types of business organisation. Make sure you look at the Int 1 notes opposite so that you are confident in being able to do this! It is useful at this level to understand what some of the different objectives mean (that is, to be able to describe them).

	Objective	What does it mean?
Private sector	• To make a profit	To have more income than expenditure/costs
	• To survive	To continue trading
	• To grow	To get bigger, for example, by opening more branches/shops
	• To offer quality goods or services	To provide a good or service at a high standard
	• To be the market leader	To have more customers than any other business in the same market
	• To have a strong brand identity	To have a well-recognised name, logo or symbol
Public sector	• To provide a service	To provide a service to other people, for example, housing, education, health facilities
	• To meet the needs of local people	To help those in the local area by improving roads, education, leisure facilities, etc in a particular location
	• To have a good image	To be seen in a positive way by other people
	• To stick to an agreed budget	To only spend the amount of money that has been allocated
Voluntary sector	• To spend donations in the best possible way	To spend donations (money) received from members of the public (donors) in the way that most benefits users of the charity
	• To promote the cause/charity	To make the cause/charity well known
	• To increase the number of volunteers	To have more people helping to support the work of the charity by, for example, working in charity shops or giving up some spare time to help
	• To increase donations	To receive more money from members of the public to help the charity's cause through fundraising activities

Quick Test 4

Intermediate 1

1. Identify two objectives for a private sector business.

2. Identify two objectives for a public sector business.

3. Identify two objectives for a voluntary organisation.

4. Define the term 'objective'.

5. Suggest an objective for a sole trader.

6. Suggest an objective for a partnership.

7. Suggest an objective for a public sector organisation.

8. Suggest an objective for a charity.

Intermediate 2

1. Describe what is meant by 'to become the market leader'.

2. Describe what is meant by 'to stick to an agreed budget'.

3. Describe what is meant by 'to increase donations'.

Stakeholders

What are stakeholders?

A **stakeholder** is anybody with an **interest** in the business being successful. They are interested in the business because they gain something from being part of it. For example, employees receive wages. Stakeholders can **influence** the way a business behaves and what it does.

Key Concepts

Different **stakeholders** have different interests in a business and can influence it in a number of different ways.

Top Tip

Stakeholders have different interests in businesses and can influence them in a number of different ways.
Interest – why they want the business to be successful.
Influence – what action a stakeholder can take to change the way a business behaves and what it does.

Some stakeholders are **internal** and some are **external**.

Internal Stakeholders *People within the business*	External Stakeholders *People outwith the business*
Owners (or shareholders), employees, managers	Customers, suppliers, government, banks, local community

The different interests and influences of each type of internal and external stakeholder are given in the table below:

Stakeholder	Interest	Influence
Owners (or shareholders)	• They get some of the profits.	• They can invest more or less capital.
Employees	• They want good wages. • They want good working conditions.	• They can take industrial action, for example, strikes.
Management	• They want bonuses and other 'perks', for example, company cars.	• They make decisions every day.
Customers	• They want to pay a good price for the product they buy. • They want to receive a good quality product.	• They can shop elsewhere.
Suppliers	• They want to be paid for the materials they provide. • They want the business to come back to them again.	• They can increase the prices they charge.
Banks	• They want loans to be repaid on time.	• They can refuse to provide loans.
Local community	• They want jobs in the local area. • They do not want the business to pollute or harm the local environment.	• They can complain to their council. • They can protest.
Government	• It wants taxes to be paid. • It makes sure the law is being followed.	• It can change the amount of tax paid. • It can introduce new laws.

Explaining stakeholder influence

You need to make sure you are able to identify **internal** and **external** stakeholders as well as being able to describe the **interest** and **influence** of each one.

At Intermediate 2 you might also be asked to **explain** the influence of a stakeholder on an organisation. What you need to add to your answer so that you have explained it is highlighted in red in the table below.

Stakeholder	Influence explained
Owners (or shareholders)	• They can invest more or less capital into the business which could allow or not allow it to expand.
Employees	• They can take industrial action (for example, strikes) which could result in lower productivity and lost orders.
Management	• They make decisions every day that could have negative consequences for the business if they are poorly made.
Customers	• They can shop somewhere else resulting in lower profits for the business
Suppliers	• They can increase the price they charge resulting in higher costs and lower profits for the business.
Banks	• They can refuse to provide loans which could result in the business suffering a cash flow problem.
Local community	• They can complain to the council, giving the business a bad image and poor reputation. • They can protest which would worsen its image and reputation.
Government	• It can change the amount of tax paid which would increase the amount of expenses the business has. • It can introduce new laws for the business to follow which could be costly for the business. The business could also face large fines if it does not follow the new laws.

Quick Test 5

Intermediate 1

1. Identify three internal stakeholders.
2. Identify three external stakeholders.
3. Describe the interest of employees.
4. Describe the interest of customers.
5. Describe the influence of employees.
6. Describe the influence of customers.

Intermediate 2

1. Explain the influence of an employee.
2. Explain the influence of a supplier.
3. Explain the influence of a customer.

Finance in business

Sources of finance

Businesses need finance (money) to be able to perform different activities. They might need finance to build new factories, to open new shops or to pay bills. Different **sources of finance** are available to businesses to help them pay for things.

Common sources of finance are bank loans, loans from family/friends, government grants and, in the case of a limited company, the issuance of more shares. Some sources of finance are not suitable for all types of businesses (for example, a loan from family or friends would not be suitable for a Plc).

Source of finance	Description	Advantages	Disadvantages
Bank loan	Loan of money from a bank repaid over time with interest	• Usually easy and quick to get • Payments can be made over a long period of time	• Interest has to be paid
Loan from family or friends	Loan of money from family or friends that does not normally have interest added	• Normally no interest has to be paid	• Arguments might occur between family/friends
Government grants	Money from the government that usually has conditions attached to it	• Do not need to be paid back	• Could take a long time to get
Issuing shares	Selling more shares to new or existing shareholders	• Large amounts of money can be raised.	• Can be expensive to issue shares

More sources of finance

In addition to the sources of finance in the table above, there are other sources available to busineses.

Source of finance	Description	Advantages	Disadvantages
Mortgage	Loan of money used to purchase property or land, repaid with interest	• Can be taken over a long period of time (for example; 25 years)	• If interest rates rise, the monthly repayment amount may increase.
Hire purchase	Where you buy an item now and pay for it later over a period of time	• Large amounts of money do not need to be spent immediately	• The item is not owned by the organisation until all payments are made.
Bank overdraft	Taking more money out of a bank account than has been put in	• Can be easy to arrange	• A large amount may not be available. • Expensive due to high interest rates charged

Some of the different methods of finance are only suitable for a **short-term** period and cannot be used to fund **long-term** investments or expansions. Short-term sources include a bank overdraft and hire purchase.

Explaining advantages and disadvantages

You might be asked to **explain** the advantages and disadvantages of different sources of finance. This means you have to give a reason why something is an advantage or a disadvantage. Taking the different sources of finance given, what you need to add to your answer so that you have explained it is highlighted in red in the table below.

Source of finance	Advantage explained	Disadvantage explained
Bank loan	• Usually easy and quick to get which means money can be accessed if needed quickly or in an emergency. • Payments can be made over a long period of time and this saves the business having to pay out a large sum of money in one go.	• Interest has to be paid which makes the loan more expensive and therefore more is repaid than has been received.
Loan from family or friends	• Normally no interest has to be paid so it does not cost the organisation anything to obtain.	• Arguments might occur between family/friends that could be stressful and cause problems if they want the loan to be repaid quickly.
Government grants	• Do not need to be paid back and therefore the business does not need to worry about how to fund repayments.	• Could take a long time to get which is not helpful if money is needed quickly.
Issuing shares	• Large amounts of money can be raised that could be used to help expand the business or purchase new fixed assets.	• Can be expensive to issue shares which is costly to the organisation.
Mortgage	• Can be taken over a long period of time (for example, 25 years) and this saves the business having to pay out a large sum of money at one time.	• If interest rates change, the monthly repayment amount changes which can make budgeting more difficult.
Hire purchase	• Large amounts of money do not need to be spent immediately saving the organisation money in the short term.	• The item is not owned by the organisation until all payments are made and the hire purchase company could claim the purchase back if payments are missed.
Bank overdraft	• Can be easy to arrange and useful if needed to cover short-term cash flow problems.	• A large amount may not be available which makes this method unsuitable for large purchases or investments.

Quick Test 6

Intermediate 1

1. Name four sources of finance.

2. Describe a bank loan.

3. Describe an advantage of a bank loan.

4. Describe a government grant.

5. Describe an advantage of a government grant.

Intermediate 2

1. Identify two sources of short-term finance.

2. Explain an advantage of a bank loan.

3. Explain a disadvantage of a bank loan.

Changes in business

What influences business?

Many things influence and impact upon how a business operates. Things happening within the business and outwith the business can impact upon decisions that are made and what the business does.

- **Internal factors** are those things **within** a business that impact upon how it works.
- **External factors** are those things **outwith** the control of a business that impact upon how it works.

Internal factors

Each **internal factor** has been listed below and the impact it has on business is given in *italics*.

- **poor management** – *the business may be poorly controlled and wrong decisions might be made*
- **poorly-trained staff** – *staff might not be able to work machinery or equipment properly and this could result in poor quality products being made or accidents happening*
- **little or no finance** – *new equipment or machinery cannot be bought*
- **poor stock-control** – *it costs more to replace stock that has gone missing or is not accounted for*
- **poor decision-making** – *wrong decisions could be costly for the business*
- **machinery or equipment breakdown** – *machinery or equipment that breaks down costs money to be fixed, and also production stops until it is fixed again*

External factors

Each **external factor** has been listed below and the impact it has on business is given in *italics*.

- **introduction of new laws** – *the business might have to provide more training to staff or provide new facilities or safety equipment*
- **changes in interest rates** – *payments, for example, on loans, could be higher or lower depending on whether the rate goes up or down*
- **increased competition** – *the business could lose customers if competitors charge lower prices*
- **fall in demand** – *a fall in demand means the business will have fewer sales*
- **changes in weather** – *some raw material, for example, fruit, might be damaged if the weather is poor; or, if the business sells ice cream and the weather suddenly gets very hot, demand could increase very quickly*
- **changes in cost of, for example, raw materials** – *this could make it more expensive and less profitable for the business to make a product*
- **introduction of new technology** – *new equipment might have to be bought which could be expensive and staff training might have to be provided*

Internal factors

The internal factors impacting upon a business are those identified above for Int 1. However, at Int 2 you should be able to explain the impact that these might have on the business and to do this you have to link the factor with the impact it has. Impacts/explanations are highlighted in red in these examples:

- Poor management results in the business being poorly controlled and wrong decisions might be made.
- Poorly-trained staff might not be able to work machinery or equipment properly and this could result in poor quality products being made or accidents happening.

Top Tip
You need to think about the impact and consequence each internal factor has on a business.

External factors

Top Tip

Any question on external factors is asking you to recall what you know about PESTEC.

Any external factor can be grouped under one of the following headings – Political, Economic, Social, Technological, Environmental or Competition. To remember this, you just need to remember the letters PESTEC. This is a good mnemonic to help you remember the external factors.

We can put the external factors from Int 1 under the appropriate headings as shown below. More examples have also been added.

Political	Economic	Social
• Introduction of new laws • Changes in the amount of tax to be paid	• Fall in demand (fewer people buying goods) • Changes in the interest rates charged by banks	• Changes in fashion/trends • Changes in working practices
Technological	**Environmental**	**Competition**
• Introduction of new technology for communication • Growth of e-commerce	• Changes in weather • Increased awareness of recycling • Pressure to reduce carbon emissions	• Increased competition

At Int 2, you should be able to explain the impact external factors have on businesses. To do this you have to link the factor with the impact it has. Impacts/explanations are highlighted in red in these examples:

* **Introduction of new laws** will mean that the business might have to provide more training to staff which could be expensive.

* **A fall in demand** will mean that fewer customers are buying a product, which results in fewer sales and lower profits.

* **Changes in interest rates** might mean that customers have less money to spend, and sales and profits could go down.

* **Changes in fashion/trends** will require the Marketing Department to carry out more research to ensure the business is providing customers with what they want, if it is to make a profit.

* **Growth of e-commerce** will require the business to invest in new technology and training to ensure it does not miss out on revenue from online shopping.

Quick Test 7

Intermediate 1

1. Name two internal factors that impact upon a business.

2. Name two external factors that impact upon a business.

3. Describe the impact of poor management on a business.

4. Describe the impact of a change in interest rates on a business.

Intermediate 2

1. Identify the term that can be used to remember the external factors.

2. Give an example of an economic factor.

3. Give an example of a social factor.

4. Explain the impact of new laws on a business.

5. Explain the impact of increased competition on a business.

Growth

Why grow?

An aim of a business may be to **grow** (to get bigger). It does this:

- to increase sales and profit and the return on the owners' investment
- to increase market share or to become market leader
- to take advantage of economies of scale (the benefits of being big)
- to reduce risk
- to become better known and gain a better reputation.

Multinationals

A multinational organisation is one that operates in more than one country. For example, it might operate in the United Kingdom and in China.

There are many advantages and disadvantages of a multinational organisation including:

Advantages	Disadvantages
• Labour might be cheaper • Production costs might be lower	• Language barriers • Different international laws

Benefits of growth

The **explanations** of the benefits of growth are highlighted in red:

- to increase sales and profit and therefore the return on the owners' investment (for example, higher dividend payments for shareholders)
- to increase market share or to become market leader which will result in more customers, higher sales and higher profits
- to take advantage of economies of scale and receive discounts on bulk buying, therefore reducing costs
- to reduce risk because a bigger business is at less risk of a takeover by a rival company
- to become better known and gain a better reputation in the market-place which will encourage new customers to buy, increasing sales and profit

Top Tip
Explanations require reasons why something is an advantage or a disadvantage.

Multinationals

The **explanations** of the advantages and disadvantages of multinationals are highlighted in red:

Advantages	Disadvantages
• Labour might be cheaper in foreign countries resulting in lower costs and higher profits. • Production costs might be lower which results in higher profits and less finance required to purchase raw materials. • Market share can be increased because the business has access to a larger market and more customers.	• Language barriers could make communication difficult and lead to decisions being wrongly implemented. • Different international laws could make trading more difficult and expensive, reducing profitability.

Methods of growth

Businesses can grow in a number of different ways. The table below gives a description of the most common methods of growth.

Method of growth	Description
Takeover	One larger business takes ownership and control of a smaller one.
Merger	Two businesses of approximately the same size agree to become one.
Vertical integration	When businesses in a similar industry, but which operate at different stages of production, join together. This can be further defined into: • **backward vertical integration** – taking over a supplier, e.g. a fish wholesaler taking over a fisherman. • **forward vertical integration** – taking over a customer, e.g. a fish wholesaler taking over a fish and chip shop.
Horizontal integration	Two businesses providing the same service, making or selling the same product, join together.
Diversification	Two businesses that provide completely different services or sell different goods from each other join together. It is also known as **conglomerate integration**.
Franchise	A person who starts a business and provides a product or service supplied by another business is known as a **franchisee** and operates a business known as a **franchise.** The franchisee is allowed to use the **franchisor's** business name and sell its products. There are advantages and disadvantages of franchising, both to the franchisor and the franchisee. **Explanations** of the advantages and disadvantages of franchising are highlighted in red:

Advantages to the franchisor	Disadvantages to the franchisor
• Franchisee provides money (usually a percentage of turnover) each year. This is guaranteed income for the franchisor. • Risk is shared between the franchisee and franchisor and if the business does not work the cost of failure is shared/split.	• The money received from the franchisee may be less than the amount the franchisor could have made themselves and is only a share of the profit made by the franchisee. • The franchisor's business name and image could be damaged as a result of a poor franchisee which could cause selling problems for the business as a whole.

Advantages to the franchisee	Disadvantages to the franchisee
• They are able to set up business using an already established name and brand that could gain customers and sales quickly compared to setting up a new business from scratch. • Cost of advertising nationally is paid for by the franchisor and therefore this cost does not need to be paid by the franchisee.	• The franchisee may have little control over products and price which could result in lost creativity and new ideas. This could be frustrating for the franchisee. • It can be expensive to purchase and set up a franchise and a potential franchisee may be unable to afford to do so.

Quick Test 8

Intermediate 1

1. List two reasons why businesses grow.

2. Define the term 'multinational'.

3. Define the term 'economies of scale'.

Intermediate 2

1. Describe what is meant by a takeover.

2. Describe what is meant by a merger.

3. Distinguish between backward and forward vertical integration.

4. Describe what is meant by a franchise.

Information in business

Where does information come from?

Information is a very important resource in business. It is used to help plan for the future and to make decisions, but where does it come from? It comes from a number of different **sources**: internal, external, primary and secondary sources.

> Remember, Int 1 material is in **blue** boxes.

> Int 2 students need to read the **blue** boxes **and** the **green** boxes.

Internal information	External information
This is information gathered from the organisation's own records. It comes from within the business. Examples: staff records, sales figures, final accounts, minutes from meetings	This is information gathered from outwith the business. Examples: newspapers, competitors' websites, government reports
Primary information	**Secondary information**
This is new information that has been gathered by the business for a specific purpose. Examples: questionnaires/ surveys, interviews, observations	This is old information that was gathered for a different purpose. Examples: information from textbooks, internet websites, newspapers

Types of information

Information comes from different **sources** (as above) and can be of **different types**.

> **Top Tip**
> **Sources** of information and **types** of information are different.

Written	This is information that is written down as text and can be read at a later time if needed. *Examples: letters, memos, reports, emails, text messages*
Oral	This is information that is spoken and heard by someone else. *Examples: telephone conversations, interviews, meetings, presentations*
Pictorial	This is information presented through photographs or pictures. *Examples: photographs, pictures*
Graphical	This is information presented through a graph or chart. *Examples: bar graphs, line graphs, pie charts*
Numerical	This is information presented through numbers which you could use to carry out different calculations. *Examples: numbers in spreadsheets, final accounts, sales figures*

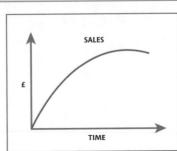

Quality of information

At Int 2, you need to be able to **describe** and **explain** the advantages and disadvantages of each source and type of information. Explanations are highlighted in red in the table below.

Top Tip
If you are asked to **'distinguish'** between two sources of information, you need to point out the differences.

Sources of information		
	Advantages	**Disadvantages**
Internal	• Unique to the organisation and is more relevant to the decision being made or the task in hand • It is known where the information has come from so it is therefore more reliable than external information	• May not be up-to-date or complete which means a wrong decision could be made • Costly computer systems might be needed to store the information which would impact upon the organisation's profitability
	Advantages	**Disadvantages**
External	• Easy to obtain and usually cheap saving the organisation money/time on carrying out research which would impact upon profitability • More information can be accessed compared to internal information using ICT which allows for a better understanding of the external business environment and better decision-making	• The source of the information might not be known and the information could therefore be unreliable • The information might be out-of-date meaning it is of a poorer quality and perhaps no longer relevant for the required purpose
	Advantages	**Disadvantages**
Primary	• Source of the information is known and is more reliable than secondary information • Information is gathered for a specific purpose so is more relevant and purposeful to the decision being made	• Can be time-consuming and expensive to collect which means the money cannot be spent on anything else (for example, purchasing a new fixed asset)
	Advantages	**Disadvantages**
Secondary	• Easy to obtain and usually cheap saving the organisation money/time on carrying out research which would impact upon profitability	• As it was collected for another purpose it is not as reliable as primary information and might not be as useful • The information might be biased which could lead to wrong or incomplete decisions being made

Types of information		
	Advantages	**Disadvantages**
Written	• Can be kept as a record for reference later which can be useful if a fact needs to be confirmed or checked • Written facts can be passed on to another person more accurately compared to oral information which results in more reliable information being communicated	• Questions and/or clarification cannot be sought which means if there is confusion over something, this cannot be clarified or checked
	Advantages	**Disadvantages**
Oral	• An instant response is given meaning decisions can be made more quickly • Questions and/or clarification can take place immediately which means if there is confusion over something, this can be resolved	• Points can be misinterpreted or misunderstood which might result in wrong decisions being made

	Advantages	Disadvantages
Pictorial	• Information is presented more attractively and is therefore more likely to be noticed by the intended users • Points can be **highlighted** which results in emphasis being placed on certain pieces of information	• Detailed or complex information cannot be communicated and this might be necessary to enable the user to fully understand a decision being made • Factual information cannot be communicated as easily as written information and this could result in facts being misunderstood or misinterpreted
	Advantages	**Disadvantages**
Graphical	• **Can make comparisons easily** and therefore decisions based on these can be made more easily • **Complicated information can be presented clearly** which means the user can understand it more easily	• The user needs to be able to interpret graphical information and they might not have the numeracy skills or ability to be able to do this
	Advantages	**Disadvantages**
Numerical	• **Financial information can be analysed** which can help in making decisions • **Calculations can be carried out using formulae** more accurately than by hand	• **Training might need to be given so that the user can carry out calculations** which could be expensive and time consuming

Quantitative and qualitative information

Information can be categorised as **quantitative** or **qualitative.**

Quantitative information is factual information that can be measured or counted. *For example, the number of people who attended a meeting was 8 or total cost of the new factory was £10,000.*

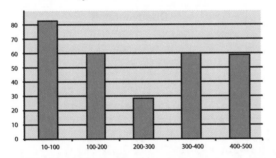

Top Tip
Be able to distinguish between and give examples of quantitative and qualitative information.

Qualitative information is information in the form of opinions or views. *For example, I didn't like the taste of the sandwich, or the colour of the new product is too dark.*

Quick Test 9

Intermediate 1

1. State the difference between sources and types of information.
2. Give an example of primary information.
3. Give an example of graphical information.
4. Describe what is meant by primary information.
5. Describe what is meant by pictorial information.
6. Describe what is meant by oral information.
7. Describe what is meant by graphical information.

Intermediate 2

1. Explain a benefit of primary information.
2. Explain a benefit of secondary information.
3. Explain a benefit of internal information.
4. Explain a disadvantage of external information.
5. Explain a benefit of written information.
6. Explain a benefit of oral information.
7. Explain a benefit of graphical information.
8. Distinguish between quantitative and qualitative information.

Use of information

Use of information in business

Information is all around us and is used every day in business. It can be used for a variety of purposes:

- to make decisions
- to monitor costs
- to check employee work rate
- to monitor how well the business is doing
- to identify new business opportunities
- to check how much profit is being made.

Top Tip
Different stakeholders use information for different reasons.

Users of information

User	Why would they use information?
Owners	• To check how much profit the business is making and what return they will receive on their investment
Management	• To check the performance of the business and how successful decision-making has been
Creditors	• To check if the business is making a profit so that they can receive payment
Employees	• To check if the business is making a profit so that they can argue for a pay rise or better working conditions
Competitors	• To check prices, product information, special offers/deals to see if they need to change their own
Customers	• To check the price of the product before deciding to buy or not
Local community	• To check whether the business will be creating new jobs in the future

Use of information in business

At Int 2, you will need to think more thoroughly about the ways that information is used in business.

Planning

Planning means thinking ahead and about the future. It involves using information to inform new plans or in making predictions and decisions about what may happen in the future.

Monitoring and control

This involves using information to check how well the business is doing. Once this has been done, it may involve making decisions to improve performance.

Decision-making

Information is used by managers to help them make decisions. Often decisions are based on ranges of information. High quality information is essential in decision-making as it helps to ensure the right decisions are made. If poor quality information is used, there could be serious consequences for the business.

Measuring performance

Information is used to check the financial performance of a business. For example, information on actual sales performance can be used to measure whether the business is meeting its sales targets. This information can be used to make a comparison with previous years' performance or against the performance of competitors by carrying out ratio analysis.

Identifying new business opportunities

Businesses can use information to see where there are opportunities to meet the needs and wants of more customers by coming up with a new business idea and then developing it. Information gathered from market research (for example, from surveys) will be particularly useful.

Quick Test 10

Intermediate 1

1. Identify four uses of business information.

2. Identify four users of business information.

3. Describe why management use information.

4. Describe why employees use information.

5. Describe why citizens use information.

Intermediate 2

1. Describe the role of information in planning.

2. Describe the role of information in monitoring and control.

3. Describe the role of information in identifying new business opportunities.

ICT in business

Use of ICT in business

ICT stands for Information and Communications Technology. A range of ICT is used in business today for a number of different reasons:

- to help with decision-making
- to collect, store and distribute information
- to communicate with customers and other stakeholders
- to maintain records.

Different types of ICT (pieces of hardware and software) are used in business to carry out some of the tasks identified above. It is important to realise that ICT is more than just using computers – it includes a wide range of other technology.

Key Concepts

What's the difference between hardware and software?

- Hardware: items which can be seen and touched, such as monitors, mice and printers.
- Software: instructions in computer languages which tell the computers how to work, for example, word processing packages.

Computer hardware

A computer system consists of different pieces of hardware and you will probably have used all or some of these in school/college or at home.

Monitor	A monitor is a screen that you look at when using a computer. It displays information which you can read.
Mouse	A mouse is used to move the **cursor** (the pointer/arrow) around the screen. You can then click on the program that you wish to use.
Keyboard	A keyboard contains keys that are used to type in letters, numbers and symbols, and to tell the computer to do certain things (for example, delete, move page down, etc).
Printer	A printer is used to make a paper copy of what is on the computer monitor. For example, a document that has been typed in a word processor could be printed out so that a hard copy is available.
Scanner	A scanner creates an electronic copy of a document that is in paper form.
Speakers	Speakers allow the computer user to hear sound, for example, music, through the computer.
Modem	A modem is used to connect a computer to the internet. It works by linking the computer through a telephone line to the internet.

Because computer systems are complicated and can hold huge ranges of information, most businesses will take a **backup** copy of their information. This means taking a copy of all the information, files and programs on the system and keeping it secure just in case something happens to the original version. For example, if a virus destroyed all the information held on a computer system, the backup copy could be used to restore the information that was stored previously.

Software

Usernames and passwords

Sometimes to use a computer you need to enter a **username** and a **password**. A username is a unique piece of information that identifies someone as the user of the computer and the password confirms that the correct person is accessing the computer. A password should be a special piece of information that nobody should be able to guess – only the user of the computer should know the password. A good password contains both letters and numbers.

Word processing

Word processing software allows text to be entered, edited and presented to suit the user's needs. It could be used to create letters, reports, memos, posters or newsletters.

	A	B	C	D
1	Sarah's Newsagents - Sales Figures			
2	Product	April	May	Total
3	Newspapers	£500	£520	£1,020
4	Magazines	£450	£540	£990
5	Milk	£100	£130	£230
6	Bread	£80	£80	£160
7	Sweets	£70	£60	£130
8	Other	£600	£700	£1,300

Spreadsheet

Spreadsheet software allows numerical information to be stored, calculated, recalled and edited. It can be used to store financial information (for example, sales figures) or stock levels. Spreadsheet software can use many formulae typed in by the user to tell the software what information the user would like. Graphs and charts can also be produced which can be useful in presenting information.

Database

Database software allows a collection of related information to be stored, recalled and edited. It can be used to

Sarah's Newsagents - Employee Details						
Employee No ·	Firstname ·	Surname ·	Address ·	Town ·	Postcode ·	Date Started ·
1 Mary	Wylie	1 Woodford Fields	Crossways	DH1 1BC	5 September 2010
2 Iain	Knox	2 Lancefield Crescent	Shieldhall	SH1 3DA	12 March 2009
3 Jean	Flett	200 Meadowside Quay	Harbourton	HB12 5TT	25 June 2008

store information about customers, employees or suppliers. Database software can hold a huge quantity of information which can be easily sorted, searched and presented in a number of different ways depending on what is required.

Presentation software

Presentation software allows presentations to be created and shown electronically, usually through a projector onto a screen. Presentation software can make presentations look much more professional and interesting by, for example, adding in animations and sound.

Top Tip
You should be able to suggest a business use for each software package.

Quick Test 11

Intermediate 1

1. Give three uses of ICT in business.
2. Give three examples of pieces of hardware.
3. Describe the purpose of a monitor.
4. Describe the purpose of a scanner.

5. Describe a spreadsheet package.
6. Describe what is meant by a 'password'.
7. Describe what is meant by a 'backup'.

The internet

The internet has changed the way people communicate, do business and generally live their lives. For example, people can now use the internet to order their shopping and have it delivered to their homes!

To access the internet, you need to have certain pieces of hardware and software. You need a computer, a modem, a telephone line and internet browsing software (for example, Internet Explorer). Descriptions of the pieces of hardware required are given on page 38.

In business, the internet can be used:

- to sell products online (This is known as e-commerce.)
- to order products online from suppliers
- to send emails to customers and other stakeholders
- to create websites
- to do internet or online banking
- to check what competitors are doing by looking at their websites.

Top Tip

Online shopping is popular. There are costs and benefits of this.

Some advantages and disadvantages of the internet are:

Advantages	Disadvantages
• Products can be sold worldwide 24 hours a day, 7 days a week, 365 days of the year.	• Staff require training.
• Access to a vast range of information	• Cost of subscribing to an internet service provider
• Communication is easier and quicker through the use of email than, for example, by post.	• Cost of making and maintaining websites
	• Staff might waste time on the internet by looking at non work-related websites (such as social networking websites).

Most businesses today have a website; a website is a collection of information in one place which can be seen by typing a website address (a URL – uniform resource locator) into a browser (a program such as Internet Explorer). A URL looks like this:

http://www.companyname.co.uk

A business may have a website to sell products, to show product information, such as prices, to display its opening hours and to provide directions to where it is based.

There are benefits to a business in having a website, such as:

- reaching customers worldwide at any time of day
- cutting down costs (such as rent of shop)
- collecting information about customers
- advertising and promoting the business.

Electronic mail

Email is used to send electronic messages to other people via their email addresses (for example, name@business.co.uk) from electronic mailboxes. It can be used to communicate with customers, other staff or suppliers who may be located all over the world.

Advantages	Disadvantages
• The same email can be sent to more than one person quickly. • Documents and files can be 'attached' to emails. • Emails can be sent worldwide instantly at little cost.	• Staff may require training. • Viruses can be spread through email. • Lots of junk or 'spam' email can be received. • Work time could be lost if staff use email for personal use.

Video conferencing

Video conferencing is when a computer link is set up between people in different locations that allows them to see and hear each other.

Hardware, such as monitors, microphones and speaker systems, is used to see and hear the people who are participating in the video conference. Video conferencing is often used to hold meetings between groups of people who are in different locations.

Advantages	Disadvantages
• Saves time and money on travelling • Allows for face-to-face communication without being in the same place	• Staff require training • Cost of purchasing hardware and software • Equipment might not work or might break down

Quick Test 12

Intermediate 1

1. Name three pieces of hardware or software required to access the internet.

2. Describe what is meant by a URL.

3. Suggest three pieces of information that might be on a website.

4. Suggest three reasons why a business might have a website.

5. Define the term 'email'.

6. Define the term 'video conferencing'.

7. Give two disadvantages of ICT in business.

Electronic diary

An electronic diary is like any other diary, but is available through a computer system. The user can enter, edit and remove different appointments (for example, meetings) as necessary. Many businesses now use electronic diaries instead of paper-based ones. Electronic diaries are very common in, for example, doctors' and dentists' surgeries. To use an electronic diary you need to have access to a computer and the appropriate software.

Advantages	Disadvantages
• Appointment reminders can be set. • Regularly occurring appointments can be entered. • Other people's diaries can be searched quickly.	• Staff require training. • Cost of purchasing software. • Diaries can't be checked if the computer system fails.

Local area network (LAN)

A LAN is a group of computers that are linked together. These computers may be in different locations but are used to share information and even pieces of software and hardware. Your school or college will probably have a LAN; you can log in (using a username and password) at different locations and still access the same files and folders. You will probably be able to print to the same printer as other people in the same location or even in different locations.

Advantages	Disadvantages
• Software can be shared. • Hardware (such as printers) can be shared. • Documents can be shared using a 'shared folder' that is accessible by all employees.	• Staff may require training. • Cost of purchasing hardware and software • Viruses could spread across the network and data could be lost.

Mobile technology

The use of mobile telephones (or 'M' technology) is now very common in business. Mobile phones can be used to carry out a range of tasks, such as making telephone calls (and leaving voicemails), sending text messages, playing games and accessing the internet. Some mobile phones are so advanced that they let you record videos, take photographs and carry out a huge range of other tasks. At the time of writing, an airline was beginning to let you use your mobile phone to board aeroplanes if you have a particular program installed on it that could display your boarding pass!

Advantages	Disadvantages
• Instant communication at any time • Voicemails can be left if a person is unable to receive a telephone call. • A range of tasks can be carried out. (For example, pictures can be sent.)	• A signal is required to make a telephone call and send text messages. • Staff training may be required. • Some mobile phones are very expensive to purchase and run.

Tablet computers

Tablet computers (such as iPads) are the most recent piece of technology to enter into the business and administrative world. They are keyboard-less computers that let users perform many of the same tasks and functions as normal laptops or desktop PCs would. Tablet computer sizes range from 5 inches to 10 inches, making them very small and portable.

Advantages	Disadvantages
• Lightweight so can be carried out more easily compared to a laptop	• Not suitable for keying in long documents

ICT at Intermediate 2

Questions on ICT are common and will come up in the internal and/ or the external assessment. You should therefore make sure you are very familiar with the content of this topic at Int 1. Questions at Int 2 will ask for more detail than at Intermediate 1 and could ask you to explain the benefits and costs of different ICT used in business.

Try writing the following benefits and costs as explanations.

Top Tip
A general summary of the benefits and costs of ICT is given here as this is a very common topic.

Benefits	Costs
• Data and information can be processed much more quickly than by traditional methods. • Improved decision-making as more information can be accessed • Lower employee wage costs if technology replaces employees • Communication between departments, branches and customers can improve through, for example, email. • Better work rates and higher productivity can be achieved.	• Can be expensive to install and maintain hardware/ software • Employees require training in using technology. • Employees may be reluctant to use new technologies and production could suffer. • Employees may feel unvalued and less motivated if they feel technology is replacing their jobs or parts of their jobs. • Technology can break down and have faults; this is costly not only in terms of getting it fixed, but also in terms of time. If production stops, the organisation's output also stops. • Many laws govern the use of ICT. (See page 107.)

Quick Test 13

Intermediate 1

1. Describe the purpose of an electronic diary.
2. Give an advantage of an electronic diary.
3. What do the letters LAN stand for?
4. Describe what is meant by a LAN.
5. Suggest three uses of a mobile telephone.

Intermediate 2

1. Describe three benefits of ICT.
2. Describe three costs of ICT.

Making decisions

Role of management

Decisions are made in business to achieve objectives. These decisions are made by managers who have the authority to make them. Decision-making involves choosing the best option from a range of options. Managers have various functions to carry out when making decisions.

Remember, Int 1 material is in **blue** boxes.

Int 2 students need to read the **blue** boxes **and** the green boxes.

Key Concepts

Decision-making – choosing an option from a range of options. This involves making a choice about which option to select and which ones to ignore.

Planning
They must plan for the future using the range of information available.

Organising
They must organise necessary resources, human and financial.

Controlling
Ensuring everything is carried out according to the plan.

Functions of managers

Co-ordinating
This involves ensuring all resources are in place to achieve plans.

Commanding
They ensure duties are carried out satisfactorily in the specified way by giving instructions.

People who are in management positions have very important roles to perform in the organisation and will have been selected based on the skills and qualities that they have.

Managers must be able to work well with other people, review and assess different situations and, where necessary, make decisions to ensure the organisation meets its objectives.

Types of decision

Managers are involved in making different types of decision.

Strategic	**What are they?** They are long-term decisions that are concerned with the overall direction, purpose and focus of the business. **Who makes them?** Strategic decisions are made by the senior management of a business. **Examples** • Expand into a foreign country (growth) • Diversify into new products • Maximise sales • Improve the image and reputation of the business
Tactical	**What are they?** They are medium-term decisions that are concerned with actions to achieve strategic decisions. **Who makes them?** Tactical decisions are made by the middle management of a business. **Examples** • Find cheaper suppliers of raw materials in order to cut costs • Expand range of goods or services offered to grow the business • Seek opportunities to sell goods or services in locations where they don't already • Develop a new marketing campaign to raise awareness of the business's products
Operational	**What are they?** They are short-term decisions which affect the day-to-day running of a business. **Who makes them?** Operational decisions are usually made by low level managers (for example, supervisor, department manager, team leader) but employees may also be involved in making them. **Examples** • Train staff in new products available • Decisions on staff working hours for next week

The decisions that managers make will help an organisation achieve certain objectives. For example, deciding to expand the goods or services offered is a tactical decision and would help to achieve the strategic objective of growth and profit maximisation. It may also contribute to achieving an increase in market share.

Top Tip
Practise **comparing** different types of decisions. You should think about what they are, who makes them and be able to give examples.

Quick Test 14

Intermediate 2

1. Outline the role of the manager in decision-making.

2. Describe what is meant by a strategic decision.

3. Give an example of a strategic decision.

4. Describe what is meant by a tactical decision.

5. Give an example of a tactical decision.

6. Describe what is meant by an operational decision.

7. Give an example of an operational decision.

8. Give three examples of skills or qualities a manager should have.

Decision-making model

What is it?

A structured decision-making model can be used by management when making decisions. It provides a framework, or a series of stages, that are followed in a sequential order.

P

Identify the problem
This means identifying the problem or issue that needs to be resolved.

O

Identify the objectives
This means considering the objective(s) that need to be achieved when making the decision.

G

Gather information
This means gathering information from a variety of sources (primary and secondary) to aid the decision-making process.

A

Analyse the gathered information
This means looking very carefully at and questioning the information that has been gathered.

D

Devise possible solutions
This means making a list of all possible solutions to the problem or issue.

S

Select the best solution
This means choosing the best solution from the range of possibilities.

C

Communicate the decision
This means letting people (for example, employees and other stakeholders) know what decision has been made.

I

Implement the decision
This means taking action to put into practice the solution that has been chosen.

E

Evaluate the effectiveness of the decision
This means thinking about how successful the decision has been. Changes might need to be made to improve it.

Costs and benefits

There are **benefits** to a business of using a structured decision-making model such as POGADSCIE.

- No quick decisions are made because time is allocated to gathering information.
- Time is given to think about and consider the range of options (alternatives) available.
- Different factors that may impact upon the decision can be considered provided time permits.
- The effectiveness and impact of each decision is considered during the evaluation stage.

However, there are also **costs**.

- It takes time to gather information and it might be difficult to obtain good quality information.
- The impact of each solution cannot be fully seen when options are being considered.
- It may be difficult to think of different solutions to complicated or unusual problems.
- Instinct and gut reactions of managers to situations are stifled because they are following a sequential process.

Quick Test 15

Intermediate 2

1. What mnemonic can be used to remember the stages of the structured decision-making model?
2. How many stages are there in the structured decision-making model?
3. Identify the stages of the decision-making model.
4. Describe three benefits of a decision-making model.
5. Describe three costs of a decision-making model.

What is an organisation?

Study note

Internal organisation will not appear in your internal assessments (NABs). It will, however, appear in your preliminary examination and also in the final SQA examination.

What is an organisation?

An organisation is a group of people who come together for a common purpose, aim or goal. Organisations will organise themselves internally to best suit the type of work they are doing.

An **organisation structure** shows how an organisation is structured and will often be presented as an **organisation chart**.

> **Top Tip**
> Marks are sometimes available for drawing an organisation chart in questions on organisation structures.

Key Concepts

Organisation charts show how an organisation is structured and how people in different departments within the organisation interact.

An organisation chart shows:

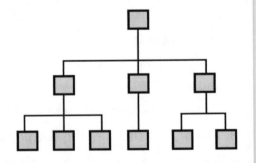

- who has overall **responsibility** for the organisation
- the levels of **authority** and **responsibility** within the organisation
- the lines of **communication** and the **chain of command**
- the **span of control** within the organisation
- different **relationships** between people within the organisation.

Key terms

You may come across many terms when learning about organisations and how they are structured. Some of the most common terms are given below.

Term	Definition
Span of control	The number of subordinates (people) who report to a person. A wide span of control will mean that many people report to one person and a narrow span of control will mean that very few people report to one person. **Wide span of control** **Narrow span of control**
Chain of command	This shows how instructions are passed down through an organisation. A long chain of command may mean communication and decision-making take longer compared to a short chain of command.
Authority	This means having the power to make decisions and to take particular actions.
Responsibility	This means being answerable for decisions and actions taken.
Delegation	This means giving the authority and responsibility to carry out a particular task or action to someone else.

Tall and flat structures

Hierarchical

These are traditional structures with many layers of management and therefore a long chain of command.

They are sometimes referred to as 'tall' structures. Instructions and decisions are passed down while information flows down and up. These structures tend to be found in large organisations such as the army or the police force.

Flat

Flat structures contain few layers of management and therefore a short chain of command.

Communication can occur more quickly within a flat structure compared to a hierarchical structure and information can flow around more easily and quickly. This type of structure tends to be found in smaller organisations, for example, a dentist's surgery.

Functional structures

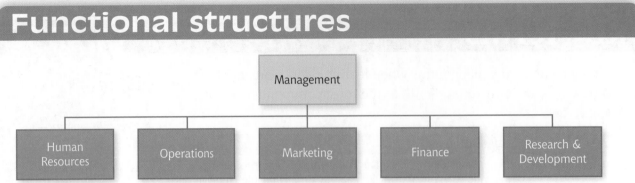

Many organisations are grouped by functional areas (departments), e.g. Human Resources, Operations, Marketing, Finance and perhaps Research & Development. People working within these departments will carry out similar tasks. Examples of tasks carried out in functional areas are given below.

Human Resources	Operations
• Recruitment and selection of staff across the organisation • Arranging training for staff • Advising on terms and conditions • Reviewing employee pay structures • Maintaining HR policies • Maintaining employee records	• Manufacturing new products • Distributing products • Ordering raw materials from suppliers • Using different methods to ensure high quality products are produced • Managing stock levels
Marketing	**Finance**
• Deciding what to produce and sell • Conducting market research • Advertising and promoting products • Deciding how much to charge for each product • Deciding upon the best way to get the product to the customer	• Receiving and processing requests for payments (i.e. bills) • Arranging for the payment of employee wages • Preparing budgets • Preparing final accounts • Carrying out financial analysis using ratios

There are different advantages and disadvantages of having a functional structure.

Advantages	Disadvantages
• Specialisation occurs as employees in the same functional area have similar skills and interests and this can have benefits for the business. • The structure of the organisation is clear to everybody (employees and visitors).	• Employees can become demotivated and bored with repeating similar tasks on an ongoing basis. • Disagreements and conflicts between different functional areas can occur if one is seen to be treated better than another (for example, allocated more money than another area).

Quick Test 16

Intermediate 2

1. Identify four functional areas.
2. Define the term 'organisation'.
3. Describe the purpose of an organisation chart.
4. Describe a functional structure.
5. Distinguish between a tall structure and a flat structure.
6. Define the term 'span of control'.
7. Define the term 'responsibility'.
8. Define the term 'authority'.
9. Define the term 'delegation'.
10. Define the term 'chain of command'.

Organisation structures

Interaction and relationships within an organisation

Look at the following organisation chart.

North Glasgow Manufacturing Ltd
ORGANISATION CHART

Communication

An organisation structure shows the **formal** lines of communication that take place and the route that is taken for information and instructions to reach a particular place. Despite the existence of formal structures (such as the organisation structure for North Glasgow Manufacturing Ltd shown above), **informal** structures (sometimes referred to as 'grapevines') can exist. Informal structures exist when communication takes place in ways that are not seen by looking at the formal organisation structure.

Top Tip
Try comparing the features of a formal and an informal structure.

Relationships in organisations

Line relationships

These are relationships between superiors and their subordinates. *For example, the Managing Director (Lee Coutts) has line relationships with the Finance Manager (Gemma McNeill), the Human Resources Manager (Lis Adams), the Operations Manager (Rena Craig) and the Marketing Manager (Anne Gillies).*

Lateral relationships

These are relationships between people on the same level of the organisation structure. *For example, the Human Resources Manager (Lis Adams) has a lateral relationship with the Operations Manager (Rena Craig).*

Functional relationships

These exist when one department provides support or a service to another department. *The Human Resources Department, for example, has a functional relationship with other departments when it provides support during the recruitment and selection process.*

Changing the structure

Organisations may decide to restructure for a number of reasons, but they mainly do so to keep up with changing business environments. Organisations must respond to changes in their business environments and, where necessary, change their organisation structures to suit current business climates. The management of an organisation has the responsibility of ensuring that the structure of the organisation meets its purpose. Organisations can change their structures by **delayering or downsizing**.

> **Top Tip**
> Make sure you know the difference between **delayering** and **downsizing**.

Delayering means changing from a tall (hierarchical) structure to a flat one by removing various levels (or layers) of management. Delayering allows for quicker communication between levels and decision-making to filter down more quickly. It can allow the organisation to adapt to changing market conditions when necessary. Delayering will allow the organisation to save money on the salaries of managers. However, the workload for existing staff could increase, which may demotivate them. Because managers will have larger spans of control, the management and supervision of staff can be more difficult.

Delayering
Removing management levels to create a flatter structure

Organisations can also change their structures by **downsizing**. This requires an organisation to remove some of its activities, for example, a branch, factory or division, from its structure. It may reduce the scale of its operations because of a decrease in demand. Some activities may be **outsourced** to other organisations to enable the organisation to concentrate on its core activities. The organisation that carries out the activity on behalf of an organisation that is downsizing will be paid for doing so and this could be expensive. It also means that the organisation needs to trust the organisation to which it outsources to deliver on time and to the standard required. Effective communication between the two organisations is crucial to the success of outsourcing.

Quick Test 17

Intermediate 2

1. Define the term 'grapevine'.
2. Describe a lateral relationship.
3. Describe a functional relationship.

4. Define the term 'outsourcing'.
5. If an organisation changes its structure by removing some of its activities, what type of restructuring is this?

What is Marketing?

The role of marketing

Marketing is a very important part of what a business does. **It involves trying to meet the needs and wants of customers so that the organisation sells its products and makes a profit.** It is more than just trying to advertise a product or selling it at the highest price.

Businesses try to produce products that are demanded by consumers (customers) in a **market**. A market is a place where buyers and sellers come together. Buyers give sellers money in exchange for goods or services. (See page 14.) A market could exist in a shop, over the internet, at a car boot sale, over the telephone or by post.

Marketing is important for a number of reasons:

- It can attract new customers.
- It can increase the amount of profit a business makes.
- It can allow the business to enter new markets.
- It can help the business grow.
- It can help the business survive.

The Marketing Department in a business carries out a number of tasks, such as finding out what customers want, advertising products, researching what competitors are doing and deciding the prices of products. These tasks are detailed in this chapter.

> Remember, Int 1 material is in **blue** boxes.

> Int 2 students need to read the **blue** boxes **and** the green boxes.

The role of marketing

Marketing can help a business increase its **market share** and become the **market leader**.

Market share – the proportion of customers that a business has in a market.
Market leader – the business that has the most customers in a market.
Market growth – increase in the number of customers buying a good or service from the business.

Market share of supermarkets in 2010

The graph shows the market share for UK supermarkets in September 2010.

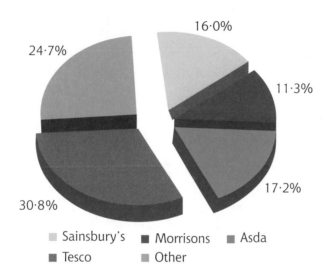

- Sainsbury's
- Morrisons
- Asda
- Tesco
- Other

Tesco was the **market leader** with a **market share** of 30·8%. If this figure grows even further, for example, to 32%, this shows that Tesco is achieving **market growth** (i.e. the number of customers buying from Tesco is increasing).

The activities that a Marketing Department undertakes must be planned and carefully carried out in order to help a business achieve its objectives, such as to increase market share, achieve growth or maximise sales. Marketing is referred to as a **strategic activity** because it impacts upon the whole business and its vision. The aims of a business will be closely linked with its marketing activities.

Businesses will produce goods or services because they think they are the best at producing them and face little or no competition **(product-led)** or because they have carried out **market research** and have identified opportunities to satisfy customers' needs **(market-led)**.

Product-led – a business produces a product because it thinks it is the best at producing it and faces little or no competition.
Market-led – market research has identified a need for a product and the business produces it to satisfy this need.

The marketing mix

The **marketing mix** consists of the **4 'P's**.

These are **product, price, place** and **promotion**.

Think of the marketing mix like baking a cake: you need the correct quantities of each ingredient before your cake will turn out the way it should. Successful marketing needs the correct quantities of each 'P'.

Top Tip
Businesses must get the correct balance between different elements of the marketing mix.

Element	Description	Why is it important?
Product	This is the actual item (good or service) the business produces and sells.	Customers will not buy something they do not want. The organisation must carry out **market research** to identify what customers want.
Price	This is how much a business charges for its product.	Customers will not buy a product if it costs too much. The price must not be too high compared to the competition because customers will buy competing products if it is. Price must reflect the product quality and the demand for it but, at the same time, allow the business to cover its costs and make a profit.
Place	This is the way the business gets the product to the customer and where it is sold.	Customers need to be able to access the product; place ensures the product is available to customers in the most accessible way. Businesses sell their products in various places including shops, internet websites, mail order catalogues and on television.
Promotion	This is how customers are made aware of the product and the ways they are encouraged to buy it. (It's more than just advertising!)	Customers need to be aware that a product exists and why they should buy it. Businesses use promotion to encourage customers to buy a product.

Top Tip
Questions on **identifying** and **describing** each element of the marketing mix are common!

Quick Test 18

Intermediate 1

1. Suggest two tasks carried out by the Marketing Department.

2. Identify the four elements of the marketing mix.

3. Give two reasons why marketing is important.

4. Define the term 'promotion'.

5. Define the term 'price'.

6. Explain why promotion is important.

7. Explain why price is important.

Intermediate 2

1. Define the term 'market share'.

2. Define the term 'market leader'.

3. Define the term 'market-led'.

4. Define the term 'product-led'.

Product

Product life cycle

Product is the actual item (good or service) the business produces and sells. Product is important because customers will not buy something they do not want.

Every product has a life cycle; it shows the stage at which the product is in its life. The diagram below shows the four stages of the product life cycle. These are **introduction, growth, maturity** and **decline**.

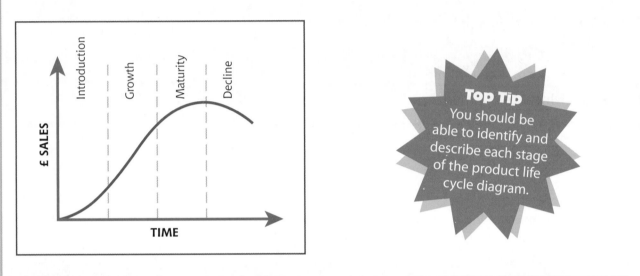

Top Tip
You should be able to identify and describe each stage of the product life cycle diagram.

Stage of the product life cycle	Description
Introduction	This is when the product is first introduced or 'launched' to the market.
Growth	This is when sales of the product are growing.
Maturity	This is when sales of the product reach their highest point.
Decline	This is when sales of the product begin to decrease because the product is older and a newer product has replaced it.

Product life cycle

At Int 2, you need to know about the six-stage product life cycle.

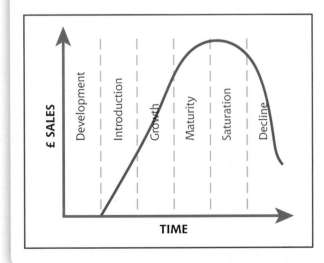

Top Tip
If you are asked to describe the stages of the product life cycle, draw a diagram to support your answer.

Stage of the product life cycle	Description
Development	During this stage, the product is developed. This might involve testing the market's reaction to the new product and/or producing a prototype (a model) of what the finished product would be.
Introduction	This is when the product is first introduced or 'launched' to the market. During the introduction stage, the product will be advertised and promoted heavily and sales will slowly increase.
Growth	This is when sales of the product are growing quickly because customers are aware that the product exists.
Maturity	This is when sales of the product reach their highest point and are most profitable for the business.
Saturation	This is when sales of the product begin to decrease because the product has saturated or flooded the market and customers no longer demand it.
Decline	This is when sales of the product decrease because the product is older and a newer product has replaced it. It will eventually become obsolete.

Businesses aim to keep products at the maturity stage for as long as possible because this is when they are most profitable. To do this, they have to 'inject' new life into products to keep them selling. There are a number of ways they can do this: these are called **extension strategies**.

Descriptions of some extension strategies are given below. In order to **explain** each strategy, what you need to add to your answer is highlighted in red.

- Change the appearance of the packaging as this gives the product a new image and will appeal to customers.

- Change the product, for example, its size, variety or shape, as this makes the product different from the original version and customers will feel they are getting something newer.

- Improve the quality of the product, for example, by using higher quality raw materials, as this will improve the way the product is seen by customers, giving it a better image.

- Change the way the product is promoted, for example, offer a 20% discount, as this will encourage customers to buy it as they are getting it cheaper.

- Change the method of advertising the product, for example, by advertising it on TV, as this will make a larger number of people aware of the product.

Top Tip
Give examples where you can on each extension strategy. Do not just write 'change product' – you must say how, for example, change its size or introduce a new variety.

Quick Test 19

Intermediate 1

1. Identify the four stages of the product life cycle.

2. Define the term 'product life cycle'.

3. Define the term 'product'.

4. Explain why product is important.

Intermediate 2

1. Identify the six stages of the product life cycle.

2. Describe what happens at each stage of the product life cycle.

3. Describe what is meant by an extension strategy.

4. Explain three strategies that could be used to extend the life cycle of a product.

What is a brand?

The name, symbol or logo given to a group or type of product is known as its **brand**. A brand makes one product or group of products different from competitors' products. Examples of common brands are Cadbury, McDonald's and Heinz.

A business has a brand to try to beat competition, to encourage repeat purchases and to try to increase market share. This can all help increase the amount of profit that the business makes.

Advantages and disadvantages of branding

Explanations of the advantages and disadvantages of branding are given below.

Advantages of branding	Disadvantages of branding
• Brand loyalty can be established with customers, which will lead to repeat purchases. • Branded products are often associated with quality and customers may be more likely to purchase them because of this. • Higher prices can often be charged and this can result in higher profits. • Brands are easily and quickly recognised by customers, helping customers to distinguish them from similar competitors' products. • New products with the brand name can be introduced successfully as the name is already well-known.	• Poor brands can have serious consequences for the business as customers may associate the whole product range with poor quality and not buy these products. • Brands can be copied and fake products can be produced and sold to try to give the impression they are the real item. • It is time-consuming and expensive for a business to establish a brand and this will impact upon the business's profitability.

Market segments

Businesses might focus their products towards a specific group of people. This is known as their **target market** or **market segment**.

Their market segment could be based on gender, income, occupation, age, social class or religious belief. For example, they might market their product towards men only. This would be an example of gender market segmentation.

Key Concepts

Market segment – the group of people or type of person a business focuses its products towards.

Market segments

Businesses might focus on a particular market segment for a number of reasons. These include:

- specific market segments can have products tailored to requirements
- prices can be set to reflect the market segment, e.g. higher prices could be charged
- not wasting money on promoting products to the wrong market segment
- products can be sold in the most appropriate place for the market segment and where they are most easily accessed.

The market can be segmented in some of the following ways:

Gender	Some products are marketed towards only men or women. *For example, certain perfumes are focused towards only men or only women as are some hair products.*
Age	Some products are marketed towards people in certain age groups. *For example, some holiday packages and destinations are marketed towards a particular age group (such as Club 18–30 holidays).*
Income/ Social class	Some products are marketed towards people who have high incomes and/or who belong to a particular social grouping. *For example, luxury sports cars, luxury holidays or cruises*
Religious belief	Some products are marketed towards people who have specific religious or cultural beliefs. *For example, particular clothing or food*
Geographical location	Some products are marketed towards people who live in particular locations. *For example, very warm clothing for people who live in particularly cold countries!*
Occupation	Some products are marketed towards people who have a particular occupation (job). *For example, stethoscopes are aimed at doctors and nurses.*

Example of market segmentation by gender

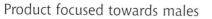

Product focused towards males

Product focused towards females

This is an example of one company producing two variations of a product (perfume): one for men and one for women.

Quick Test 20

Intermediate 1

1. Identify four ways in which a market could be segmented.

2. Define the term 'branding'.

3. Identify two benefits of branding.

4. Define the term 'market segment'.

Intermediate 2

1. Describe three benefits of market segmentation.

2. Explain two advantages of branding.

3. Explain two disadvantages of branding.

Price

What is price?

The price is how much a business charges for its product. The price charged by a business is important because customers will not buy the product if it costs too much. The business also wants to cover the cost of making the product and make a profit.

The price must not be too high compared to the competition because customers will buy competing products if it is. It must reflect the product's quality and the demand for it but, at the same time, allow the business to cover its costs and make a profit.

Top Tip
You should be able to identify and describe different pricing strategies.

A business prices its products depending on the **pricing strategy** that it has chosen.

Pricing strategy	Description
Low price	The price charged is lower than competitors' prices.
High price	The price charged is higher than competitors' prices.
Penetration pricing	The price charged is lower than competitors' prices when the product is first launched to encourage people to buy it.
Price skimming	The price charged is high because the product is new and often unique. Customers are happy to pay a high price because they will be the first ones to own the product.
Destroyer pricing	The price charged is very low (lower than competitors' prices) to force competitors out of the market because customers will not purchase from them.

Pricing strategies

At Int 2, you should be able to **describe** and **justify** different pricing strategies.

Pricing strategy	Description	Justification
Low price	The price charged is lower than competitors' prices.	Customers will buy the product because it is cheaper than competitors' products.
High price	The price charged is higher than competitors' prices.	Customers will buy the product because they perceive it to be of a higher quality than competitors' products.
Penetration pricing	The price charged is lower than competitors' prices when the product is first launched to encourage people to buy it.	This strategy will allow a business to attract customers from their competitors because its product is cheaper. Once customers have been attracted, the price is then increased.
Price skimming	The price charged is high because the product is new and often unique. Customers are happy to pay a high price because they will be the first ones to own the product.	A high price can be charged due to no or little competition and because of the uniqueness of the product. A large profit can be made. The price can be lowered at a later date if competition enters the market.
Destroyer pricing	The price charged is very low (lower than competitors' prices) to force competitors out of the market because customers will not purchase from them.	This destroys competition. Once this happens, the price will then be increased and customers will buy it as there is no alternative supplier of the product.

Loss leaders	Selling the product at a price lower than it costs to make it.	Attracts customers to the business. Customers hopefully purchase other products at the same time that are normally priced. The business will make a profit based on the overall cost to the customer of the products purchased.
Cost-plus pricing	A percentage of profit is added onto the cost of making the product.	The cost of producing the product is covered and an element of profit is built into the price.

How do businesses decide the price?

The price of the product is very important, especially when introducing a new product to the market or when attempting to extend the life cycle of a product. Businesses have various factors to consider when setting a product's price:

- the product's life cycle position
- how much competitors charge for their product
- the cost of making the product or providing the service
- the level of profit that is wanted
- the market segment that the product is focused towards
- how much of the product can be supplied.

Businesses need to think carefully about what price to charge. Certain pricing strategies are only for use in the short term, some are only for exclusive items and some can be used in the long term.

Price skimming, for example, can be used for unique and exclusive products, as this strategy sets a higher price and customers are often willing to pay the higher price because of the exclusiveness of the product. In competitive markets, destroyer pricing can be used in the hope it will remove competition from the market and therefore leave the business as the only supplier of the product.

Businesses constantly review the prices they charge because they operate in environments that do not stand still. Changes in demand because of external factors are common, as is pressure from customers for low prices. Competitors are also doing their market research and trying to introduce products that will be better and cheaper than those of their rivals.

Top Tip
Different pricing strategies are used for different types of products. Some are more suitable than others.

Quick Test 21

Intermediate 1

1. Identify three pricing strategies.
2. Define the term 'price'.
3. Suggest a reason why charging the correct price is important.
4. Describe what is meant by low price.
5. Describe what is meant by high price.

Intermediate 2

1. Justify using a low price as a pricing strategy.
2. Justify using destroyer pricing as a pricing strategy.
3. Suggest when price skimming could be used.
4. Describe three factors to be considered when deciding upon a pricing strategy.

Place

What is place?

Place consists of two things: (1) the way the business gets the product to the customer and (2) where the product is sold. Where the product is sold is known as the market; it is where the buyer and seller come together.

Place is important because customers need convenient access to the product. Customers can buy products in shops/supermarkets, online, through a TV shopping channel, over the telephone and through the post.

Channels of distribution

Top Tip
The channel of distribution always starts with the **manufacturer** and ends with the **customer**.

A **channel of distribution** is the *route* a product will follow to get from the manufacturer to the customer. A product can take one of several routes as shown below.

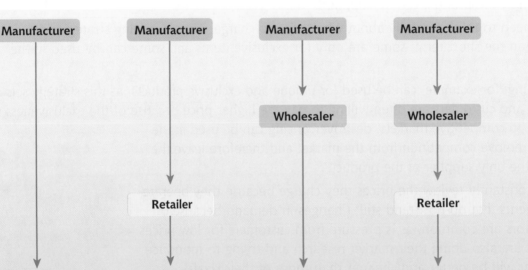

- The **manufacturer** makes the product. This might take place in a factory.
- A **wholesaler** buys large quantities of items from the manufacturer and then sells them on to retailers (or sometimes directly to customers) in smaller quantities.
- A **retailer** distributes products to customers on behalf of manufacturers.
- The **customer** is the person who purchases the product.

Top Tip
Do not confuse channels of distribution with the physical way the product gets to the customer (e.g. by road, rail, sea or air). They are different!

There are a number of factors that will determine which channel of distribution is used by a business. These factors include:

- the actual product and its life cycle
- the image the manufacturer wants the product to have
- the availability of finance
- the reputation and reliability of wholesalers and retailers.

Retailers and wholesalers

Retailers are businesses that distribute products to customers on behalf of manufacturers. Retailers stock ranges of products from a number of manufacturers and wholesalers. They will decide on the prices customers pay and will display the products in the most effective ways. Manufacturers will decide which retailers to use, based on where the customers are, and what extra services (for example, credit and delivery terms) they offer. Retailers benefit from sourcing products directly from manufacturers by being able to specify exactly what they want and at what cost. Sometimes retailers can take advantage of **economies of scale**. Sometimes, however, manufacturers do not use retailers in their distribution channels because their products will face competition in retailers' stores and because it adds an extra financial cost to the distribution channel.

Key Concepts

Economies of scale – the advantages of being a large business. For example, they are able to buy in bulk and receive discounts.

A **wholesaler** buys large quantities of items from the manufacturer and then sells them on to retailers (or sometimes directly to customers) in smaller quantities. Information on products is usually provided by wholesalers to retailers.

Quick Test 22

Intermediate 1

1. Identify three examples of a market.
2. Define the term 'place'.
3. Describe why place is important.

Intermediate 2

1. Identify four channels of distribution.
2. Define the term 'channel of distribution'.
3. Define the term 'wholesaler'.
4. Define the term 'retailer'.
5. Identify four factors to be considered when deciding upon a suitable channel of distribution.

Promotion

What is promotion?

Promotion is how customers are made aware that products exist. Promotion also encourages customers to buy products.

Products can be promoted to customers in different ways.

Promotion method	Description
Advertising (for example, on TV)	Advertising involves letting people know that a product exists and trying to persuade them to buy it. Advertising is used to inform people about the product: how much it costs and what it does. Advertising is important; otherwise, people wouldn't know that a product exists.
	For example, it could be an advert on TV or in a newspaper or magazine.
Special offers (such as, discounts)	Discounts provide customers with money off a product when they buy it. For example, they might get 20% off or if they buy one they get one free (BOGOF).
Free samples	Some businesses give out free samples or tasters of products to see if people like them. If they do like them, they might decide to buy the products.
	For example, some perfume shops give out free samples of perfumes for people to try. Without the free samples, customers might never know if they liked them!
Celebrity endorsement	A celebrity is used to promote a business and its products. For example, Jamie Oliver has been used to promote Sainsbury's.

Top Tip
You should be able to identify and describe different methods of promotion.

Advertising

Advertising communicates that a product exists. It usually includes information about the product and at the same time it encourages customers to buy it. It helps to increase sales because if customers don't know that a product exists, they can't buy it.

Top Tip
Businesses will use a range of promotion methods to obtain the biggest impact.

Internet websites	An internet website is a collection of information in one place which can be seen by typing a website address (a URL) into a program such as Internet Explorer. A business may have a website to communicate information about its products and also to sell products online; this is known as e-commerce.

Advantages	Disadvantages
• Customers worldwide can be targeted. • Customers can buy online 24/7 from a place of their choice. • Online discounts are often given. • Product information can be updated and accessed quickly. • Stock availability can be checked and items reserved before purchasing.	• Customers are unable to handle or see the goods fully. • Customers may be unwilling to disclose their personal or credit/debit card details. • There may be computer or internet problems while ordering. • The customer has no personal contact with the organisation.

A variety of things can be done to encourage people to buy online. These include offering discounts, free postage, fast delivery times and having a website that is easy to use and which offers secure payment facilities.

Businesses can use sound, graphics and video clips to make their websites more appealing and attractive.

Newspapers	Several types of newspapers are available; some are only available locally and some are only available on Sundays. There are several newspapers that are designed for specific audiences (for example, the *Financial Times* for those with an interest in business).

Advantages	Disadvantages
• National newspapers allow for an audience across the country, whereas local newspapers target people in a particular location. • Adverts can be kept by readers for use at a later date. • Depending on the advert size, a lot of information can be communicated.	• Some newspapers do not print everything in colour; this may mean an advert has less of an impact. • No sound or video clips can be shown to demonstrate how the product would function. • Could be expensive, especially in national newspapers.

Television	Television advertising has the potential to reach a large audience because many people watch television. Adverts are only shown on certain channels and between different programmes or during commercial breaks.

Advantages	Disadvantages
• Large audiences can be reached. • Adverts can be shown during particular programmes to target specific audiences who the product may most appeal to. • The product can be shown from different angles and colourful demonstrations can be given.	• Advertising nationally on TV can be expensive. • Some people tend not to watch the adverts and instead turn over to other programmes. • As adverts tend to be very short, people do not have much time to take in the advert and take note of all the product details or contact information.

There are other methods of advertising that can be used. Businesses are taking advantage of modern technology (such as text messaging) to promote their products as well as using more traditional methods such as mailshots through the post, radio advertising and billboards.

Celebrity endorsement

Businesses often pay celebrities to promote their products to the public. This is known as **product or celebrity endorsement**.

Advantages	Disadvantages
• Promotes a good image/name for the business. • People often want to buy products to be associated with the celebrity. • If the celebrity is successful, sales levels can be increased.	• Highly expensive method of promotion. • The correct celebrity needs to be chosen to match the image the product should have. • Any negative publicity about the celebrity can impact upon sales of the product.

Quick Test 23

Intermediate 1

1. Identify four methods of promotion.

2. Define the term 'promotion'.

3. Explain why promotion is important.

4. Describe what is meant by advertising.

5. Describe what is meant by special offers.

Intermediate 2

1. Describe two advantages of advertising on a website.

2. Describe two disadvantages of advertising on a website.

3. Describe what is meant by 'celebrity endorsement'.

Market research

What is market research?

Market research involves businesses finding out what customers want and what is happening within the markets that they operate in. It involves them looking at information that already exists and finding out new information.

There are two types of market research.

Field research	Desk research
This involves gathering new information by carrying out surveys, interviews or observations.	This involves looking at information that already exists, for example on books, newspapers and websites.

Surveys, interviews and observations are used to find out new information. (This is field research.)

- **Survey** – people are asked to answer questions about the business and its products. This might take place on the street, on the internet or over the telephone.
- **Interview** – a person is asked a number of questions by another person and gives their answers orally.
- **Observation** – a person or group of people are watched while carrying out an activity or task.

Top Tip
You should be able to **identify** and **describe** different types of field research.

Field and desk research

The advantages and disadvantages of field and desk research are given below. What you need to add to your answer to make it an **explanation** is given in red.

	Advantages	Disadvantages
Field research	• The information is gathered first hand (is new) and is more reliable than existing information. • Information is gathered for a specific purpose so is more relevant and purposeful to the decision being made.	• Can be expensive to carry out which means the money cannot be spent on anything else (such as a new fixed asset). • It is time-consuming to carry out and might take a long time to gather lots of responses to surveys, etc, which could hold up decision-making.

	Advantages	Disadvantages
Desk research	• Easy to obtain and usually cheap saving the organisation money/time on carrying out field research which would impact upon profitability. • Quick to find information on the internet and decisions can therefore be made quickly.	• As it was collected for another purpose, it is not as reliable as field research and might not be as useful. • The information might be biased which could lead to wrong and incomplete decisions being made.

Surveys

A survey (questionnaire) involves asking people their views and opinions on issues through a series of questions. It could be done in person, over the telephone or through the post. Sometimes people might be asked for their general views or they might be asked to rate certain things, for example, how much they agree or disagree with something on a scale of 1 to 5.

Top Tip
Surveys and questionnaires are the same thing.

Advantages of surveys	Disadvantages of surveys
• It is inexpensive to do compared to other methods of field research. • Large numbers of people can take part.	• People don't always like taking part in surveys and might not do it. • People might not give the correct answer; they might give the answer they think is wanted.

Postal survey – this is when people are sent questionnaires through the post. They will be asked to complete and then return the questionnaires to the organisation.

Advantages	Disadvantages
• Large numbers of people spread across a large geographical area can be surveyed at a fairly inexpensive cost. • Larger surveys can be carried out and people can complete them at their own pace at a time and place of their choosing.	• Relies on people opening the letter containing the questionnaire, completing it and then sending it back; not many people do this. • Information is not obtained instantly. • The respondent does not have the opportunity to clarify anything he or she does not understand. • The survey must be designed carefully so that it is not open to interpretation or misunderstanding.

Telephone survey – this is when people are contacted by telephone and asked to answer a series of questions.

Advantages	Disadvantages
• Large numbers of people spread across a large area can be surveyed. • It is less expensive to conduct compared to a personal interview. • The person being surveyed has the opportunity to clarify anything he or she is not sure of. • Information is obtained instantly.	• Many people do not like taking part in telephone surveys and may not do so. • Large and time-consuming surveys are unlikely to go down well and therefore this method tends to suit only short surveys.

Personal interview – this involves a face-to-face, two-way process whereby a researcher (the interviewer) will ask a person (the interviewee) a number of questions and they will respond orally.

Advantages	Disadvantages
• The researcher or person being interviewed can clarify anything he or she does not understand. • Body language and facial expressions to questions can be monitored and recorded.	• Time-consuming and expensive to carry out; not many people can be asked for their opinions in this way compared to a postal or telephone survey. • The researcher will require training in interview and questioning techniques for it to be successful.

Focus groups

A focus group is simply a discussion between a selected number of people and an experienced researcher. People will be asked for their views **(qualitative information)** on certain things and the idea is to generate a discussion on these.

Advantages	Disadvantages
• People's feelings and views can be observed.	• Qualitative information is difficult to analyse.

Hall test

A Hall test involves a product being given to customers to try and then obtaining their opinions and views **(qualitative information)** on it; they are basically being given a free trial of the product.

Advantages	Disadvantages
• Participants get to try out the product for themselves and can report back on it. • It is relatively inexpensive to carry out.	• Qualitative information (opinions and views) is difficult to analyse. • People may give the response they think the organisation wants to hear as they do not want to appear rude or ungrateful for the free trial given to them.

Observation

An observation involves watching something and recording what happens. It could be that the observer has to count how many times something happens, or someone does something, or what someone's reaction is to a particular situation.

Advantages	Disadvantages
• Quantitative information (facts and figures) is gathered which is easier to analyse than qualitative information (opinions and views). • Those being observed may be unaware so should act naturally.	• Those being observed cannot be asked their opinion or give an explanation as to why they did or did not do something.

Sampling

When businesses carry out field research, it is impossible for them to ask everyone for their opinion on something. For this reason, they have to select which people to question or, in other words, select a **sample** of people to be questioned. Different sampling methods can be used.

Random sampling	Randomly selecting people from a list, such as a telephone book or electoral roll, and then telephoning these people.
Stratified random sampling	The sample is based on segments of how the population as a whole is divided, for example, sampling only a certain group of people.
Quota sampling	Selecting a number of people to question based on certain characteristics (for example, age, occupation, gender)

Quick Test 24

Intermediate 1

1. Define the term 'market research'.

2. Describe what is meant by 'field research'.

3. Describe what is meant by 'desk research'.

4. Give three examples of field research.

5. Give three examples of desk research.

6. Describe the purpose of an interview.

7. Describe the purpose of a survey.

Intermediate 2

1. Distinguish between field research and desk research.

2. Describe three methods of field research.

3. Explain two advantages of desk research.

4. Explain two advantages of field research.

5. Describe 3 sampling techniques.

6. Describe an advantage of a focus group.

7. Describe an advantage of a Hall test.

What is Operations?

The Operations function (or department) in a business is the department that manufactures products. They turn inputs (e.g. raw materials and other resources) into outputs (the finished product). This enables the business to make a profit and to create wealth. (See page 15.)

Remember, Int 1 material is in **blue** boxes.

Int 2 students need to read the **blue** boxes **and** the green boxes.

Role of Operations

- Turning inputs into outputs by following set processes
- Meeting customer demand by supplying them with products they want
- Using production resources (such as machinery and labour) in the best possible way
- Managing stock levels
- Choosing a suitable supplier of raw materials.

Top Tip
The Operations function turns inputs (e.g. raw materials) into outputs (the finished product) by following a process
(input → process → output).

Elements of the Operations function

The Operations function transforms inputs into outputs. This is done by deciding the best way to transform raw materials and other inputs into the finished product and at the same time organising the necessary resources to do this. At all times, it is important to remember the quality of the finished product is very important.

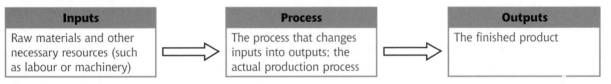

Inputs	Process	Outputs
Raw materials and other necessary resources (such as labour or machinery)	The process that changes inputs into outputs; the actual production process	The finished product

The Operations function consists of different elements. These include system design, system operation and purchasing.

System design

This element is concerned with deciding the best way to organise work (i.e. the flow or process of production). It considers the best way that products should be made and the best way to distribute products once they have been made.

System operation

This element is concerned with ensuring there are enough raw materials to keep production going. It involves making sure that there are the correct quantities of raw materials available when they are needed for manufacturing processes.

Purchasing

The purchasing of raw materials to be used in the operations process is very important. It is dealt with separately below.

Choosing a supplier

Raw materials are the basic ingredients that are used in making a product. These have to be purchased from suppliers. When a business is choosing suppliers of raw materials, it has a number of factors to take into account. These include:

- the cost of the raw materials
- the quality of the raw materials
- the time that it will take for raw materials to be delivered
- the quantity that can be delivered
- the storage space available
- how reliable the supplier is.

Purchasing raw materials

We have identified the factors that need to be considered when choosing a supplier of raw materials, but why are they important?

	Justifications (reasons why these are important)
The cost of the raw materials	• Costs need to be kept to a minimum to maximise profit. • Low costs contribute to a healthy cash flow.
The quality of the raw materials	• Without quality raw materials, the finished product will not be of a high quality. • To keep wastage to a minimum as wastage is costly to the business.
The time that it will take for the raw materials to be delivered	• Some raw materials (such as fresh food) may be perishable and need to be used quickly in the production process. • The business does not want production to stop because it is costly and delivery deadlines might not be met.
The quantity that can be delivered	• There should always be enough raw materials available to allow production to continue. However, too much will mean that they need to be stored, which could be expensive. • Quantity should never go above the maximum stock level.
The storage space available	• Storage could be expensive and the business wants to keep costs low to maximise profit.
How reliable the supplier is	• It could be costly to the business if the supplier did not deliver on time; production would need to stop and customers would not be happy if delivery times were not met.

Quick Test 25

Intermediate 1

1. Define the term 'Operations'.
2. Describe three tasks carried out by the Operations function.
3. Describe what is meant by 'raw materials'.
4. Suggest three factors to be considered when choosing a supplier.

Intermediate 2

1. Identify the three elements of the Operations function.
2. Describe each element of the Operations function.

Managing stock

Stock control

The supply of goods that a business has needs to be managed. There are three factors to control:

1. Raw materials **2. Goods currently being made** **3. Finished goods**

At all times stock levels have to be managed carefully. If a business has too much or too little stock, this could cause problems.

Problems of having too little stock	Problems of having too much stock
• Production could stop as there are not enough materials. • Customers might not receive their orders on time. • This could give a poor image which could result in loss of customers	• It could be costly (e.g. paying for storage). • Stock is at higher risk of being stolen. • Stock might become out of date.

Businesses need to have a system in place that manages levels of stock. They do this by setting a **maximum stock level, minimum stock level, re-order level and re-order quantity.**

Maximum stock level	The maximum amount of stock in the business at any one time.
Minimum stock level	The minimum amount of stock in the business at any one time.
Re-order level	The quantity at which more stock should be ordered.
Re-order quantity	The quantity of stock to be ordered from suppliers to bring the stock level back to the maximum level.

Stock can be managed using **stock record cards** or on **computerised systems**. Stock record cards are used to record levels of stock manually whereas a computerised system records stock levels automatically. The stock record card would include: the minimum stock level, the maximum stock level, the re-order level, the re-order quantity and the name of the supplier.

Storing stock

Stock should be stored in a place that is secure, well ventilated, well lit and dry. These things are important to ensure that stock remains safe and of a high quality. Stock can be stored in a centralised or decentralised location.

	Advantages	Disadvantages
Centralised storage *This means keeping all stock in one place.*	• Security is easier to install and maintain therefore theft is less likely. • Procedures for receiving, issuing and distributing stock can be easier to implement across the whole organisation.	• A dedicated area for storing stock could be expensive to set up and maintain. • Time could be wasted going to and from the storage area.
	Advantages	Disadvantages
Decentralised storage *This means keeping stock in more than one place.*	• Stock can be more easily accessed and can be easily obtained when needed. • Less chance of stock going to waste or deteriorating.	• Storage space is required in several locations. • Security is more difficult to maintain so risk of theft is higher.

Computerised stock control systems

A computerised stock control system records stock levels automatically. There are benefits and costs associated with using computerised stock control systems.

Benefits	Costs
• The system automatically reorders stock when it is required. • The system can tell quickly which products are selling well and which ones are not. (This can be useful to management in making decisions.) • A count of stock by hand is no longer required.	• The system could be expensive to purchase. • Staff require training in using the system. • Upgrades to the system might be necessary; these could be expensive.

Just in Time (JIT)

Just in Time is a method of stock control that keeps stock levels to the minimum possible. As the name suggests, stock arrives *just in time* for it to be used in the production process. Goods are only manufactured when a customer order is received.

JIT in practice requires suppliers who can deliver on time otherwise production will stop. It also requires procedures to ensure quality is maintained. Highly skilled employees are required as there are no extra raw materials available. However, it does save money being tied up in stock as well as in the storage and security of stock. There is also less chance of stock going to waste through deterioration.

Quick Test 26

Intermediate 1

1. Name the three factors to be controlled when managing stock.

2. Suggest two problems of having too little stock.

3. Suggest two problems of having too much stock.

4. Describe a stock record card.

Intermediate 2

1. Distinguish between centralised and decentralised stock storage.

2. Define the term 'Just in Time'.

3. Suggest two advantages of Just in Time.

4. Suggest two benefits of computerised stock control.

5. Suggest two costs of computerised stock control.

Types of Production

Production methods

Businesses must decide which method(s) of production to use to create their products or, in other words, how to **process** the **inputs** into **outputs.**

In deciding which method would be best to use, there are several factors that need to be considered:

- type and nature of the product being made
- quantity of the product being made
- methods used to ensure quality
- the way stock is managed
- resources (e.g. human) and technology (e.g. machinery) available.

There are three main methods of production: **job, batch** and **flow.**

Job production

This is when one product is made from start to finish before another one is made. The product is made to the customer's exact requirements, which results in unique or one-off products being made. Such products are often made by hand.

Examples: wedding cakes, pieces of art, handmade chocolates.

Advantages of job production	Disadvantages of job production
• Customers' exact demands can be met. • High prices can be charged. • Designs can be changed.	• Specialist tools or equipment may be needed. • Bulk purchases of stock are not always possible. • Products can take a long time to make.

Batch production

This is when one group of identical products is made at a time before another group of different products is made. All products in the batch move on to each stage of production at the same time. Machinery and equipment may be cleaned and/or changed between batches to produce a different product.

Examples: cakes, newspapers, bread.

Advantages of batch production	Disadvantages of batch production
• Batches can be changed to suit customers' requirements and demands. • Cost savings can be made compared to job production.	• Resources (such as equipment and employees) may have nothing to do between each batch. • A fault or error in one item can lead to the whole batch being wasted. • The cost of each item could be high if only small batches are being made.

Flow production

This is when parts are added to the product as it moves along the production line. The final product will have been manufactured by the time it reaches the end of the production line. It is sometimes called **line production**.

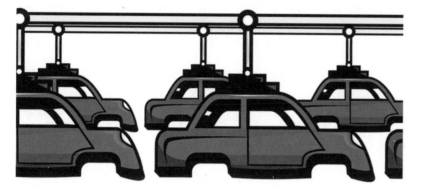

Examples: cars, computers, other electrical items.

Advantages of flow production	Disadvantages of flow production
• Large quantities of identical products can be made. • Machinery is often used for the whole production process. • Raw materials can be purchased in bulk. • Machinery can work 24 hours a day, 7 days a week.	• Products cannot be made to customers' individual requirements. • A fault or breakdown in one part of the production line could cause production to stop. • Mass demand for identical products is needed.

Automation and mechanisation

Products can be made by using a mixture of two resources: people and machinery.

Products could be made by people only	This is known as **labour intensive production**.
Products could be made by people and machinery	This is known as **mechanisation**. Mechanisation involves machinery as well as some degree of labour in the production process. For example, people may still be required to operate some parts of the machinery being used.
Products could be made by machinery only	This is known as **automation** or **capital intensive production**. Automation means that machinery controlled by computers is used instead of people to make something. It is sometimes used because machines do not require breaks and can work 24/7, unlike people.

Types of production

At Int 2, you should be able to explain the advantages and disadvantages of different types of production. What you need to add to your answer to make it an explanation is highlighted in red in the tables below.

Top Tip
'Explain' means – give a reason why.

Job production

Explained advantages of job production	Explained disadvantages of job production
• Customers' exact demands can be met resulting in a more personal service being offered and a happier customer. • High prices can be charged as customers are often willing to pay higher prices for exclusive or unique products. • Designs can be changed to suit an individual customer's requirements, even when production has begun; this gives the customer a sense of ownership over what is being made.	• Specialist tools or equipment may be needed which could be expensive to purchase and might only be used once. • Bulk purchases of stock are not always possible and therefore the business cannot make cost savings through economies of scale. • Products can take a long time to make and the employee making the product may lose motivation as a result.

Batch production

Explained advantages of batch production	Explained disadvantages of batch production
• Batches can be changed to suit customers' requirements and demands resulting in a more personal service being offered and happier customers. • Cost savings can be made compared to job production which means the organisation will become more profitable.	• Resources (such as equipment and employees) may have nothing to do between each batch which is expensive for the organisation and demotivating for employees. • A fault or error in one item can lead to the whole batch being wasted which is costly because the whole batch would need to be made again. • The cost of each item could be high if only small batches are being made and this results in a higher price having to be charged to the customer.

Flow production

Explained advantages of flow production	Explained disadvantages of flow production
• Large quantities of identical products can be made compared to job production where it could take a long time to produce only one product. • Machinery is often used for the whole production process and therefore no employees need to be paid. • Raw materials can be purchased in bulk saving the business money. • Machinery can work 24 hours a day, 7 days a week whereas people cannot as they require breaks and rest.	• Products cannot be made to customers' individual requirements and therefore customers do not get an exclusive or unique product. • A fault or breakdown in one part of the production line could cause production to stop and this means no products being produced. • Mass demand for identical products is needed as this method of production is not suitable for producing small quantities of goods and may not suit all types of products.

Labour and capital intensive

The quantity of capital (machinery and equipment) or labour (humans) used in a business determines whether it is **labour** or **capital** intensive. The advantages and disadvantages of both are given below.

Labour intensive	Advantages	Disadvantages
	• Employees can use their initiative when required. • There is always a supply of labour available. • It is cheaper than purchasing expensive equipment and machinery.	• Costly and time-consuming to recruit, select and train employees. • The accuracy and quality of work can vary depending on who is making the product.

Capital intensive	Advantages	Disadvantages
	• Machinery can work 24 hours, 7 days per week and does not require breaks. • Accuracy and quality of work are standardised (i.e. the same).	• It cannot meet individual and specific customer requirements. • Breakdowns can be costly and time consuming. • Employees become tired and bored of the repetitive tasks.

Remember!

- **Automation** means that machinery has replaced the need for employees to carry out the work required because machinery can do it instead.
- **Mechanisation** involves machinery as well as some degree of labour in the production process.

Top Tip
You could be asked to **distinguish** between labour and capital intensive production.

Quick Test 27

Intermediate 1

1. Define the term 'automation'.
2. Define the term 'mechanisation'.
3. Describe job production and give an example.
4. Describe batch production and give an example.
5. Describe flow production and give an example.

Intermediate 2

1. Explain two advantages of job production.
2. Explain two advantages of batch production.
3. Explain two advantages of flow production.
4. Distinguish between labour and capital intensive production.

Managing quality

Producing a high quality product

Producing a quality product is very important. Customers will not buy a product that is not of a high quality.

Businesses can use a variety of methods to produce quality products.

- They can use high quality raw materials from a good supplier.
- They can train their staff to a high standard.
- They can update and maintain the machinery used in production.
- They can use **quality assurance** (checking products at various stages during production).

A business which produces products to a high quality may receive a **quality standard**. For example, the BS kitemark is a symbol of quality on many products.

Importance of quality

Customers expect products to be of high quality. This means that the products work in the way they should, have been manufactured using high quality raw materials and look good. The products should be delivered on time and after sales service should be provided.

Poor quality is the exact opposite of high quality. Poor quality products do not work the way they should, may have been made with poor quality raw materials and may have poor physical appearance.

The advantages of providing a high quality product are:

- customers may make repeat purchases in the future
- a good reputation is established which encourages new customers
- customers are less likely to purchase from a competitor
- profit can be maximised
- the business can grow and increase its market share
- wastage will be minimised and the cost of production kept low.

Top Tip
Quality is important to a business and is a common topic in exams.

Methods of ensuring quality

Quality assurance	Quality assurance involves checking the product at various stages of the production process. It attempts to reduce wastage by knowing in advance the standards for each stage. Any products that do not meet the standards are discarded.
Quality control	Quality control involves checking the product once it has been manufactured. Any product which does not meet the necessary standard will be scrapped, resulting in a high level of wastage.
Benchmarking	Benchmarking involves comparing one product with another similar product, often using the market leader's standards as the benchmark. The business will attempt to match these standards.
Quality circles	Quality circles involve members of the organisation meeting regularly with management to discuss quality issues and then attempting to find ways to solve them. This involves employees at all levels of the hierarchy.

The role of other departments

Other departments in the organisation have a role to play in providing quality.

Human Resources	Marketing	Finance
• Should recruit and select appropriately skilled and qualified individuals • Should provide high quality training • Should have a system in place for recognising employees' strengths and areas for improvement (appraisal)	• Should obtain feedback from customers (market research) and, where necessary, act on this feedback • Should develop a prototype or model to show what the product would look like and test market it	• Need to provide the Operations function with enough money to purchase high quality raw materials • Advice on which suppliers are good at paying their bills should be provided

Top Tip
Other departments have an important role in helping the business provide a high quality product.

Quick Test 28

Intermediate 1

1. Suggest a reason why providing a high quality product is important.
2. Suggest four ways a business can produce a high quality product.
3. Define the term 'quality assurance'.
4. Give an example of a quality symbol.

Intermediate 2

1. Suggest three reasons why providing a high quality product is important.
2. Define the term 'quality control'.
3. Define the term 'benchmarking'.
4. Describe what is meant by a quality circle.
5. Suggest two activities that the Human Resources Department could do to contribute towards quality.

What is Finance?

Role of Finance

A business has to manage its money carefully. Money is important in order for a business to be able to achieve its objectives and to keep its owners happy. Businesses will usually have a Finance Department whose role is to manage the financial (money) side of the business.

The Finance Department in a business is responsible for managing the business's wmoney. This department has various tasks to carry out:

- **Maintaining financial records** – records of the money going out and coming into the business have to be kept.
- **Paying bills** – suppliers have to be paid on time and other bills, such as electricity, also have to be paid.
- **Paying wages and salaries** – employees have to be paid for the work that they carry out.

> Remember, Int 1 material is in **blue** boxes.

> Int 2 students need to read the **blue** boxes **and** the **green** boxes.

Importance of Finance

We have seen that the Finance Department has three main tasks to carry out:
(1) maintaining financial records, (2) paying bills and (3) paying wages and salaries.

It has to do these for a number of reasons:

- **Maintaining financial records**
  It must prepare financial statements such as budgets to help management in decision-making.
- **Paying bills**
  Bills and accounts must be paid on time to ensure the business maintains a good reputation and good relationships with its suppliers, and to enable it to maintain a good credit rating.
- **Paying wages and salaries**
  Employees must be paid the correct amounts on time. If their pay is wrong or late they may become unhappy and demotivated. Incorrect pay could impact upon personal items of expenditure (such as mortgage and household bills). It could also result in industrial action.

Uses of financial information

Financial information prepared by the Finance Department has a considerable number of uses:

- **To enable costs and expenditure to be controlled**

  Costs and expenses must be controlled to avoid financial problems and the need to borrow money to cover these costs. Where necessary, management might have to take action to reduce costs and the amount of money going out of the organisation.

- **To enable cash flow going in and out of the business to be monitored**

  Money moving into and out of the business needs to be monitored. Businesses need to have enough 'cash' available to pay bills and employees' wages. Making profit and having good cash flow are two different things.

- **To forecast what might happen in the future**

  Preparing budgets and looking at past financial records can help management identify trends and predict what may happen in the future. Where necessary, action can be taken to avoid financial problems.

- **To monitor performance**

  Financial information from one year can be compared against that from previous years and against competitors. This is useful to see if action taken in the past has worked and, where necessary, to take action in the future.

- **To provide management with information for decision-making**

  We have already discovered that management makes lots of decisions. Financial information plays a crucial role in decision-making processes and will often help management to decide which courses of action are taken.

Quick Test 29

Intermediate 1

1. Identify three tasks carried out by the Finance Department.
2. Describe the role of the Finance Department.

Intermediate 2

1. Suggest three uses of financial information.
2. Describe three tasks carried out by the Finance Department.
3. Explain why it is important that bills are paid on time.
4. Explain why it is important that employees are paid correctly.

Financial information

Sources of financial information

Financial information is recorded in different places. These include the Trading, Profit and Loss Account, the Balance Sheet and the Cash Flow Statement (Cash Budget).

Financial information	What does it show?
Trading, Profit and Loss Account	Trading Account This shows how much profit a business has made from buying materials and selling products (gross profit). Profit and Loss Account This shows how much profit a business has made, once other income and expenses have been taken into account (net profit).
Balance Sheet	This shows the value or worth of a business.
Cash Flow Statement (Cash Budget)	This is a forecast of the money that is expected to come in and go out of a business over a period of time in the future.

Trading, Profit and Loss Account

Top Tip
You won't be asked to prepare a set of accounts.

This shows a summary of the money that has come in and gone out of the business over a particular period of time (usually one year).

The **Trading Account** shows the **Gross Profit** whereas the **Profit and Loss Account** shows the **Net Profit.**

GROSS PROFIT – profit made from buying and selling goods.
This is profit before expenses are subtracted.

EXPENSES – these are items the business has to pay for.

NET PROFIT – the amount of profit made after expenses have been subtracted from the Gross Profit.

Trading, Profit and Loss Account of North Glasgow Travel for the year ending 31 December		
	£000	£000
Sales		300
Less Cost of Sales		
Opening Stock	40	
Add Purchases	150	
	190	
Less Closing Stock	20	
Cost of Goods Sold		170
GROSS PROFIT		130
Less Expenses:		
Rent	10	
Advertising	8	
Electricity	3	
Telephone	15	
Wages	10	46
NET PROFIT		84

The Balance Sheet

The **Balance Sheet** shows the value or worth of the organisation at a particular point in time. It shows what the organisation owns **(assets)** and what debts **(liabilities)** it has.

FIXED ASSETS – items owned by the business that will last for longer than one year, e.g. vehicles, premises, land, machinery.

CURRENT ASSETS – items owned by the business that will last for less than one year, e.g. stock, cash, debtors.

CURRENT LIABILITIES – these are short-term debts that the business has. (Short term means less than one year.)

DRAWINGS – money that the owners have taken out of the business for their own personal use.

Balance Sheet of North Glasgow Travel as at 31 December		
	£000	£000
FIXED ASSETS		
Premises		250
Equipment		100
Vehicles		50
		400
CURRENT ASSETS		
Closing Stock	20	
Debtors	40	
Bank	50	
	110	
Less Current Liabilities		
Creditors	25	
Working Capital		85
Capital Employed		485
Financed by		
Opening Capital		420
Add Net Profit		84
		504
Less Drawings		19
		485

DEBTORS – people who owe money to the business.

CREDITORS – people to whom the business owes money (e.g. suppliers).

WORKING CAPITAL – current assets minus current liabilities.

CAPITAL EMPLOYED – working capital plus fixed assets.

This Balance Sheet does not show any examples of **long-term liabilities**. These are debts the business has that will last for longer than one year. These could be long-term loans or a mortgage on premises.

Quick Test 30

Intermediate 1

1. Describe the purpose of a Trading, Profit and Loss Account.
2. Describe the purpose of a Balance Sheet.
3. Define the term 'Gross Profit'.
4. Define the term 'Net Profit'.
5. Define the term 'Drawings'.
6. Define the term 'Fixed Assets'.
7. Give two examples of a Fixed Asset.
8. Define the term 'Current Assets'.
9. Give two examples of a Current Asset.
10. Define the term 'Current Liabilities'.
11. Give an example of a Current Liability.
12. Define the term 'creditor'.
13. Define the term 'debtor'.

Cash Flow

Cash flow management

Cash is a very important resource in any business. It is needed to pay bills, to purchase assets and to pay employees. All businesses want to maximise profit, but they need cash on a day-to-day basis to operate.

It is important that an organisation monitors its cash flow so that it can continue to operate successfully, pay its bills and organise resources in the most efficient way. Many problems organisations face can be caused by poor cash flow.

Businesses can improve cash flow by:

- seeking cheaper suppliers of raw materials
- selling assets they no longer use or need
- increasing advertising and marketing activities
- increasing or decreasing the price of products.

Businesses face a number of expenses and these have to be managed. They have to pay various bills (such as for raw materials, electricity) and pay their employees. They can try to minimise costs by finding cheaper suppliers of raw materials, cutting overtime paid to employees and seeking cheaper sources of electricity.

Cash flow management

Failure to have a healthy cash flow can be caused by a number of reasons including:

- having too much money tied up in stock
- too much time given to customers to pay their debt (a long credit period)
- not enough money being made from sales
- too short a credit period being offered by creditors or suppliers
- the value of drawings taken out by owners has been high
- spending too much money on fixed assets and other capital items (such as machines).

Top Tip
Methods of solving cash flow problems is a common exam question.

Cash flow problems can be solved in a number of ways. Some of the problems above could be solved by:

Suggestion	Justification
Introduce a Just in Time approach to managing stock	To save money being tied up in stock. By using a JIT system, stock is only purchased when it is needed.
Offer cash discounts to customers who pay on time	This will encourage customers to pay their bills more quickly and the cash received can be used to fund other activities and pay bills.
Increase advertising and promotion activities	Advertising can raise awareness of the business and its products. Different promotion activities (e.g. special offers) could be used to entice customers to buy. More products being purchased by customers increases sales and cash flow and reduces stock levels.
Sell assets (e.g. machines) that are no longer required	Selling assets which are no longer required will generate cash and, because they are not required by the business, it will not cause any disruption to operations.
Take out a bank loan	A business could take out a loan and pay back the loan over a period of time. A loan normally has interest added.

Check the reliability of customers	Only customers who are reliable and likely to pay their bills on time should be sold products. (This method would not be suitable for a small shop.)
Increase capital from shareholders or owners	If the business is a limited company (Ltd or Plc), additional shares could be issued. This would increase the capital available to the business. Alternatively, for a sole trader or partner, the owners could invest additional capital.

NB – Sources of finance (see page 26) can also be used to solve cash flow problems.

Sources of finance (see page 26)

Top Tip
Some methods of solving cash flow problems are only for short-term use and not for the long term.

Cash budget/cash flow statements

To help manage cash and ensure control over future cash flow, businesses can prepare a **cash budget** (**cash flow statement**). This is a forecast of the money they expect to receive (**receipts**) and the money they expect to pay out (**payments**) over a period of time in the future.

The benefits of preparing a cash budget include:
* being able to see the money expected to come in and go out of the business over a period of time
* action (for example arranging additional sources of finance) can be taken when a cash flow problem is expected
* information contained in budgets can be used to make decisions.

This is an example of a cash budget.

Top Tip
A cash budget is prepared in advance. For example, the cash budget shown below for May and June might have been prepared in February.

Cash budget of North Glasgow Travel for May and June		
	May	June
Opening balance	1000	1350
Receipts		
Sales	5000	5500
Total cash	6000	6850
Payments		
Purchases	2400	1900
Wages	1200	1600
Advertising	300	280
Rent	300	300
Insurance	450	450
Other expenses		1250
Total payments	4650	5780
Closing balance	1350	1070

The cash budget shows the expected receipts (inflows) and payments (outflows) of cash over a period of time.

RECEIPTS – money expected to come in to the business

PAYMENTS – money expected to be paid out

*Look at this example .... even though sales are higher in June, the closing balance is lower than for May. This is because **payments** have been higher in June.*

Quick Test 31

Intermediate 1

1. Suggest two ways of improving cash flow.

2. Suggest two ways of reducing costs.

3. Describe the purpose of a cash budget.

Intermediate 2

1. Describe four methods of solving a cash flow problem.

2. Suggest three causes of cash flow problems.

3. Justify using JIT as a method of solving cash flow problems.

Users of financial information

Users of financial information

Financial information is used by many different stakeholders for a number of reasons. We need to identify the different users of financial information and the reasons why they are interested.

The final accounts (i.e. Trading, Profit and Loss Account and Balance Sheet) can be used to show an organisation's **profitability, liquidity** and **efficiency.** This information is gathered by carrying out ratio analysis. We will look at this on page 90.

- **Profitability** – how profitable the business is
- **Liquidity** – how able the business is to pay its short-term debts
- **Efficiency** – shows if the business is performing effectively and efficiently

Stakeholder	Interest in financial information
Management	• To see if decisions they have made have been effective • To enable planning for the future so that the business can achieve its objectives (for example, growth)
Employees	• To see whether or not the business is paying fair wages based on the profit it is making • To understand why certain decisions may be taken (such as redundancies, pay cuts) • To assure themselves that the organisation is making a profit and that their job is secure
Trade unions	• To see whether or not the business is paying fair wages based on the profit it is making. It might be possible to negotiate higher pay • If profit is good, better working conditions and other benefits could be argued for
Government	• To ensure the correct amount of taxation is being paid. This is based upon the net profit figure from the Trading, Profit and Loss Account.
Shareholders	• To decide on how to vote at the AGM (for shareholders of a Plc) • To decide whether to purchase additional shares (for shareholders of a Plc) • The current share price can be used to determine whether to sell or buy more shares • To decide whether the organisation is paying a fair dividend based on the profit made
Creditors	• Based on liquidity information, a creditor may decide to give more credit (for example, a loan or more time to pay off existing debts) • Liquidity information will show how able the organisation is to pay off its short-term debts
Local community	• To see if the business is making a profit and will survive in order to provide and protect jobs in the local area

Top Tip
Some users of financial information are internal (e.g. employees, managers) whereas some are external (e.g. government, suppliers).

Limitations of financial information

Management makes decisions and plans for the future based on financial information. However, there are limitations to this. Not all decisions can be based purely on how profitable the business is, because the majority of financial information is based on past events and is therefore old.

When judging the success of a business, financial information (and the results of ratio analysis) cannot be used on its own because the following are not shown:

- the level of staff motivation or morale
- the impact of external factors on the organisation (i.e. PESTEC)
- future product developments or plans
- how successful the organisation has been in eliminating competition
- the stage of the organisation's product in the product life cycle
- any current changes to the organisation and its structure.

Top Tip

Financial information does not reveal everything about an organisation. There are other factors which are important and need to be considered when judging how successful an organisation is.

Quick Test 32

Intermediate 2

1. Identify four users of financial information.
2. Describe the interest of management in financial information.
3. Describe the interest of trade unions in financial information.
4. Describe the interest of the local community in financial information.
5. Explain why financial information has its limitations.

Ratio analysis

What is ratio analysis?

Financial information can be analysed in more detail by carrying out ratio analysis. Ratio analysis can be used to compare an organisation's performance with that of past years and with that of similar organisations. It can help identify trends and irregularities over a period of time. Where the results of ratio analysis give cause for concern, action can be taken to try to improve the ratio.

Ratio	Interpretation	Why would it change?
Gross Profit Percentage **This ratio shows the profit made from the buying and selling of stock.** $\frac{\text{Gross Profit}}{\text{Sales}} \times 100 = - \%$ The higher the % the better. If in Year 1 the ratio was 30% and in Year 2 it was 35%, this shows that for every pound made from sales, more of it is gross profit in Year 2 than in Year 1.	If the ratio INCREASES this means more gross profit is being made from each pound of sales.	• Selling price has been raised. • Cost of sales has been lower because cheaper suppliers have been used. • Increase in sales because of better marketing or as a result of a marketing campaign.
	If the ratio DECREASES this means less gross profit is being made from each pound of sales.	• Cost of sales has increased. It would be necessary to find cheaper suppliers or negotiate discounts. • Stock has been lost due to theft or wastage. • Fewer marketing activities which has caused a decrease in sales.
Net Profit Percentage **This ratio shows the profit made once expenses have been paid by the organisation.** $\frac{\text{Net Profit}}{\text{Sales}} \times 100 = - \%$ The higher the % the better. If in Year 1 the ratio was 25% and in Year 2 it was 30% this shows that for every pound made from sales, more of it is net profit in Year 2 than in Year 1.	If the ratio INCREASES this means more net profit is being made from each pound of sales.	• Gross profit has been higher. • Expenses have been lower because cheaper alternatives (e.g. for electricity supplies) have been found.
	If the ratio DECREASES this means less net profit is being made from each pound of sales.	• Gross profit has decreased. (See reasons above.) • Expenses have increased – it would be necessary to find cheaper alternatives.
Return on Capital Employed **This ratio shows the return on the capital investment made by the owner or shareholder in the organisation.** $\frac{\text{Net Profit}}{\text{Capital Employed}} \times 100 = - \%$ The higher the % the better. If in Year 1 the ratio was 20% and in Year 2 it was 25%, this means in Year 2 you have made a return of 25%. For every £1 invested, you have made a return of 25p.	If the ratio INCREASES this means the owner or shareholder is making more of a return on their investment.	• Sales have increased because of better marketing. • Expenses have been lower because a cheaper supplier is being used.
	If the ratio DECREASES this means the owner or shareholder is making less of a return on their investment.	• Sales have decreased because of poor marketing. • Fewer sales have been made because a competitor has a better and more cost effective alternative. • Expenses have increased – it would necessary to find cheaper alternatives.

Mark Up Ratio	If the ratio INCREASES this means more profit has been made after the cost of goods sold.	• Selling price has been raised. • Cost of sales has been lower because cheaper suppliers have been used.
This ratio shows how much profit has been added to the cost of goods sold. $\dfrac{\text{Gross Profit}}{\text{Cost of Goods Sold}} \times 100 = — \%$ The higher the % the better. If the ratio was 32% in Year 1 and 37% in Year 2, that means more 'mark up' (or profit) has been added to the product. If a product cost the organisation £1 to produce and it was sold for £1.30 this would be a 30% mark up.	If the ratio DECREASES this means less profit has been made after the cost of goods sold.	• Cost of sales has increased. It would be necessary to find cheaper suppliers or negotiate discounts. • Selling price has been lowered perhaps to encourage more sales or to eliminate competition.
Current Ratio *(also called the Working Capital Ratio)*	If the ratio INCREASES this means the organisation has an increased ability to pay off its short-term debts.	• Current liabilities have decreased. • Current assets have increased.
This ratio shows how able an organisation is to pay off its short-term debts. $\dfrac{\text{Current Assets}}{\text{Current Liabilities}} : 1$ An ideal answer would be 2:1. This means it has double the amount of current assets compared to current liabilities. If the answer was 1:1 or lower the organisation would not be able to pay its current liabilities.	If the ratio DECREASES this means the organisation has less ability to pay off its short-term debts.	• Current liabilities have increased (e.g. increase in creditors). • Current assets have decreased (e.g. decrease in stock held or money in the bank).
Acid Test Ratio **This ratio shows how able an organisation is to pay off its short-term debts without having to sell its stock.** *(Stock can be difficult to turn into cash because it is least liquid.)*	If the ratio INCREASES this means the organisation has an increased ability to pay off its short-term debts.	• Current liabilities have decreased (e.g. creditors have been paid and this figure is lower). • Current assets have increased (but not the stock figure).
$\dfrac{\text{Current Assets – Stock}}{\text{Current Liabilities}} : 1$ A result of 1:1 is considered acceptable. If this was the case, it would mean the organisation could pay off its short-term debts without having to sell any stock.	If the ratio DECREASES this means the organisation has less ability to pay off its short-term debts.	• Current liabilities have increased (e.g. the amount due to creditors has increased). • Current assets have decreased (but not the stock figure).

Quick Test 33

Intermediate 2

1. Identify three ratios that could be calculated by a business.

2. Describe the Gross Profit Ratio.

3. Describe the Net Profit Ratio.

4. Describe the Current Ratio.

5. Give a reason why the Gross Profit Ratio might increase.

6. Give a reason why the Net Profit Ratio might increase.

Introduction to Human Resource Management

What is Human Resource Management?

The Human Resource Management (HRM) Department in a business deals with and manages employee-related issues. A business must look after its employees because they are a very important resource for the business in being able to achieve its objectives. Some of the activities that the HRM Department carries out are shown here.

Remember, Int 1 material is in **blue** boxes.

Int 2 students need to read the **blue** boxes **and** the **green** boxes.

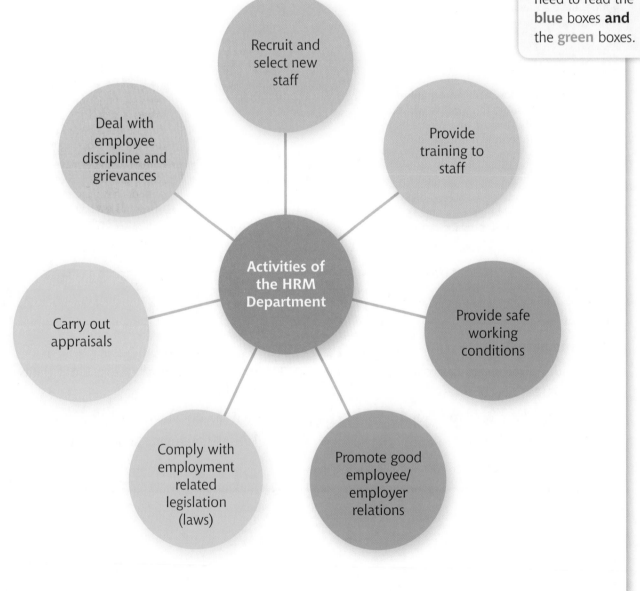

Working practices

There has been a change in where and when people work in the past 20 or so years. There has been a shift away from the traditional Monday to Friday 9am – 5pm pattern. Businesses have had to develop a range of working practices to satisfy the needs of their employees and to maintain good employee relations. They have introduced working practices such as those shown below.

Working practice	Description
Temporary contracts	Employees are employed on a casual basis and only for a short period of time to supplement the core staff already employed.
	This is commonly used when there is an increase in demand at particular times of year. At Christmas, for example, many businesses, including the Post Office and large retailers, employ people on temporary contracts to cope with the increase in demand.
Part-time contracts	People who work less than 35 hours per week. For example, they might work a couple of days per week.
Homeworking	Employees work from home using ICT to communicate with the business when necessary.
Teleworking	Employees work away from the office and use ICT to communicate with the business when necessary. For example, sales people who work away from the office but communicate regularly with the business using a range of ICT including laptops and Personal Digital Assistants (PDAs).
Flexitime	Employees are given flexibility in their starting and finishing times. They usually have to be present during 'core time' which would be set by the business.
	This allows employees to manage their work/life balance better. For example, they can take their children to school and/or avoid rush-hour traffic.
Job share	This is when two people share one full-time job.

There are benefits of having flexible working practices to both the employee and the organisation.

Benefits to the employee	Benefits to the organisation
• People can balance their personal and work commitments more easily and therefore have a better work/life balance. • Employees can choose their own own start and finishing times. • Travelling time and cost can be reduced. • It can be less stressful for employees as they are more in control of their work and personal commitments.	• Staff are generally more motivated and are therefore more productive. • There will be reduced incidences of absence and late starting. • Space and money can be saved in the office if employees are working out of the office. • Potential employees may be attracted to a business that offers flexible working practices.

Quick Test 34

Intermediate 1

1. What do the letters HRM stand for?

2. Identify three activities carried out by the HRM Department.

3. Describe the purpose of the HRM Department.

Intermediate 2

1. Define the term 'flexitime'.

2. Suggest two benefits of flexible working practices for an employee.

3. Suggest two benefits of flexible working practices for an organisation.

4. Compare homeworking and teleworking.

5. Define the term 'motivation'.

Recruitment

What is recruitment?

Recruitment means encouraging people to apply for a job vacancy. It is important that highly skilled people are attracted to work for a business because they play an important part in a business being able to provide a high quality good or service. The recruitment process has a number of stages.

Key Concepts

Recruitment – encouraging people to apply for a job vacancy.

Top Tip
Recruitment is not the same as selection. These stages take place **before** the selection process begins.

RECRUITMENT PROCESS

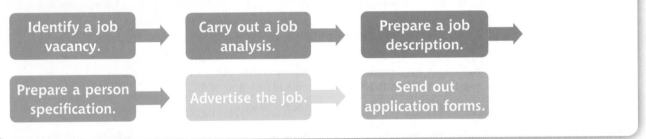

Identify a job vacancy.	→	Carry out a job analysis.	→	Prepare a job description.	→
Prepare a person specification.	→	Advertise the job.	→	Send out application forms.	

Job description

A **job description** contains information about what the job involves. An example of a job description and the type of information it would contain is shown below.

```
NORTH GLASGOW TRAVEL
Job Description

Job Title:          Administrative Assistant
Location of Job:    123 Castlebank Place,
                    Glasgow, G1 1NG
Hours of Work:      Monday to Friday, 9am to 5pm
Duties:             Opening the mail, welcoming customers,
                    answering the telephone, filing and other
                    duties instructed by the Manager
```

Person specification

A **person specification** provides information about the type of person that is required to do the job. An example of a person specification and the type of information it would contain is shown below.

NORTH GLASGOW TRAVEL
Person Specification for Administrative Assistant

Skills:	Computer and word processing skills
Qualities:	Friendly, good telephone manner, able to work on their own
Qualifications:	Qualifications in Administration and English are essential
Experience:	No experience needed

Advertising the job vacancy

A job vacancy has to be advertised. This is known as the method of recruitment. The job could be advertised in newspapers, in job centres, in shop windows, on websites or on the radio.

Application forms

An **application form** is sent out to people who are interested in applying for a job (they are known as the job applicant). It asks them questions about themselves and they are required to give answers.

The application form will ask for the applicant's name and address, past experience/jobs, qualifications and hobbies, and may ask them to write down why they want the job. The application form should always be completed neatly and in full.

Application form

X ——————

Top Tip
Application forms are increasingly being completed online to save costs.

Quick Test 35

Intermediate 1

1. Define the term 'recruitment'.
2. Identify five stages in the recruitment process.
3. Name two pieces of information on a job description.
4. Name two pieces of information on a person specification.
5. Suggest two methods of recruitment.
6. Name two pieces of information on an application form.

Recruitment

We looked at the stages of recruitment in the previous section. However, you need to be able to **describe** each stage of recruitment rather than just **identify** it.

Stage in recruitment	Description
Identify a job vacancy	This involves identifying that a job vacancy actually exists. Perhaps someone has left the business and therefore the vacancy needs to be filled.
Carry out a job analysis	This involves looking at the tasks and duties that would be carried out as part of the job. The responsibilities of the person who has the job would also be considered.
Prepare a job description	The job description contains information about what the job involves: tasks, duties, responsibilities, pay, working hours, holiday entitlement and any other benefits.
Prepare a person specification	The person specification contains information about the type of person required to do the job. Certain skills, qualifications and experience may be needed to fulfil the requirements of the job. The person specification can be used as a tool in the selection process as it provides a list of what is essential and what is desirable for a candidate to have. This can be used to assess the suitability of the applicant for the job and for the applicant to see whether or not the job is for them.
Advertise the job vacancy	The job vacancy has to be advertised. It can be advertised within or outwith the business. These are known as **internal** and **external recruitment.** *Internal and external recruitment are described below. Explanations of the advantages and disadvantages of each are also given.*

Top Tip
Questions on internal and external recruitment are common.

Internal recruitment
The job vacancy is only advertised within the organisation and therefore only those people already working for the organisation can apply for it.

Administration Manager: Woolshires

For our Edinburgh export office
Job description
Manage a busy export office
Support the Director
Supervise junior staff
Organise holiday rotas
Salary £30,000
Apply today to hr@woolshires.co.uk

Advantages	Disadvantages
• Existing employees are known by the organisation and, if chosen, the organisation can be confident that they can fulfil the duties of the post. • Employees feel more valued and can become more motivated and productive if given the chance of promotion. • As external methods of recruitment are not required, money can be saved on advertising, lowering the organisation's expenses. • Existing employees are already familiar with the organisation's policies and therefore no time or money needs to be spent on providing training.	• The opportunity to bring someone with new ideas into the organisation, who could have given the organisation a competitive edge, is lost. • There may not be an existing employee who has the skills or qualities to carry out the job and the post may go unfilled for a long period of time.

External recruitment

The job vacancy is advertised both within and outwith the organisation and therefore anyone (whether an existing employee or not) can apply.

jobcentreplus

Advantages	Disadvantages
• People with fresh ideas, who can inject new thinking and energy into what the organisation is trying to achieve, can be brought into the organisation. • It can attract large quantities of applicants which means the organisation has a wider selection of people to choose from.	• Existing employees who apply but do not get the job may feel unvalued and therefore lose motivation to work hard. • It can be expensive to advertise in a range of external places and therefore the cost of external recruitment could be high. • No matter how good the selection methods are, because the person is unknown, there is a chance that the wrong person could be chosen and the job could be carried out poorly.

Send out application forms	Application forms are sent out to people who are interested in applying for the job. The form asks the applicant about themselves and why they want the job. The applicant then sends back the application form to the organisation.

Quick Test 36

Intermediate 2

1. Describe the purpose of a job analysis.

2. Distinguish between internal and external recruitment.

3. Explain two advantages of internal recruitment.

4. Explain two advantages of external recruitment.

5. Explain two disadvantages of internal recruitment.

6. Explain two disadvantages of external recruitment.

Selection

What is selection?

Selection means choosing the best person for the job from those who have applied. Once the business has received all the completed application forms, it then has to begin the **selection process**.

> **Key Concepts**
>
> **Selection** – choosing the best person for a job.

Top Tip
Many **documents** are used in the recruitment and selection processes.

Selection process

Application forms compared against person specification

See page 95 for more information on these.

↓

References checked

A **reference** is a report about a person from a previous employer or from a school/college.

↓

A shortlist of candidates for interview is created.

A **shortlist** contains the people who are thought to be suitable for the job based on their application and references.

↓

Interviews are carried out.

An **interview** is a meeting between an applicant and people from the business. The applicant is asked questions about the job and why they want it.

↓

Other tests might be carried out.

For example – applicants for an administration job might be asked to do a typing **test** to see if they are suitable.

↓

The best candidate chosen and told he or she has been successful.

The successful candidate is told first because if they decide not to take the job, it would then be offered to the next suitable candidate.

↓

Those who did not get the job are told and may be given feedback.

Top Tip
Every organisation will use a range of selection methods.

Applications, CVs and references

Organisations can use one or more methods of selection to choose the right person for a job. The different selection methods aim to assess the suitability of each applicant against the person specification.

Applicants for a job are usually required to send in a completed **application form** and/or **curriculum vitae** (CV) together with **references.** There can be hundreds of people applying for one job and it would be impossible and expensive to consider all of these further by interviewing them all or using other selection methods. Instead, the organisation can read through each individual applicant's application form or CV and references and decide who to take to the next stage of the selection process. This is known as **shortlisting.**

Top Tip
The more selection methods used the greater the chance of selecting the best person for the job.

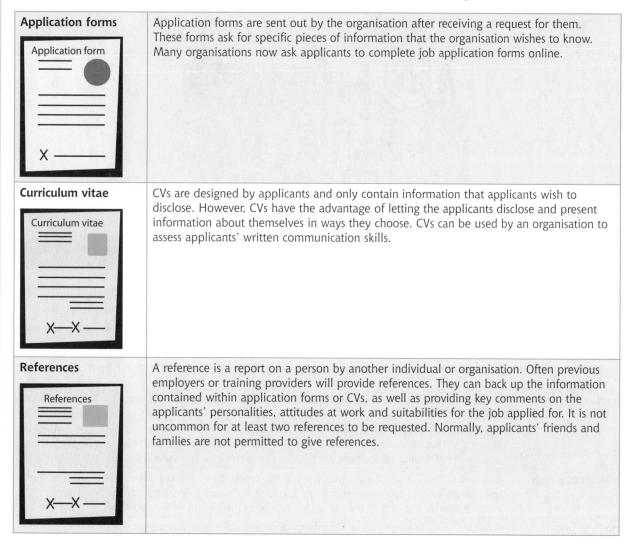

Application forms	Application forms are sent out by the organisation after receiving a request for them. These forms ask for specific pieces of information that the organisation wishes to know. Many organisations now ask applicants to complete job application forms online.
Curriculum vitae	CVs are designed by applicants and only contain information that applicants wish to disclose. However, CVs have the advantage of letting the applicants disclose and present information about themselves in ways they choose. CVs can be used by an organisation to assess applicants' written communication skills.
References	A reference is a report on a person by another individual or organisation. Often previous employers or training providers will provide references. They can back up the information contained within application forms or CVs, as well as providing key comments on the applicants' personalities, attitudes at work and suitabilities for the job applied for. It is not uncommon for at least two references to be requested. Normally, applicants' friends and families are not permitted to give references.

Interviews

An **interview** is a meeting between the applicant and people from the organisation. The applicant is asked questions about the job and why they want it.

Advantages	Disadvantages
• The applicant's personality and appearance can be assessed. • The applicant can be asked questions about the content of their application form or CV. • The applicant has the opportunity to ask questions about the job.	• Some people can perform very well at interviews but in reality they might not be the best person for the job. • Some interviewers may be biased towards certain applicants. • It's a time-consuming process.

Testing

A variety of tests can be carried out to help in the selection process. Each test will assess a different aspect of the applicant and can provide useful information as well as confirming the information given on the application form, CV or at interview. However, tests are expensive and time-consuming for organisations to carry out. Testing needs to be carried out with caution because, just like exams, people can perform worse than expected because of the stress imposed on them.

Psychometric tests	In these tests, applicants are asked questions which will assess their personality. These tests can be used to find out what type of person they are and whether they suit the requirements of the job. Unlike some other tests, there are no correct answers and applicants should give truthful answers so that accurate pictures of their personalities can be built up. However, applicants do not always give the real answers but the ones they think an organisation would want to hear.
Intelligence tests	Also known as IQ tests, these assess the mental capability of the applicant. Questions in these tests centre around problem-solving and thinking skills, numeracy and literacy. Each applicant is given a score at the end of the test which can be compared to other applicants.
Medical tests	A doctor or nurse examines applicants for any medical issues or concerns that may impact upon their ability to perform the duties of the job. Some occupations (such as the emergency services and the army) require strict medical conditions to be met.

Assessment centres

Assessment centres allow organisations to see applicants undertake varieties of tasks in different situations. Such assessments often take place over a couple of days. Many large organisations have assessment centres where job applicants take part in role-play exercises and team-building activities and make presentations. At all times during assessments organisations will be watching applicants carefully and making notes of their communication, teamwork and problem-solving skills.

Quick Test 37

Intermediate 1

1. Identify three methods of selection.

2. Define the term 'selection'.

3. Describe the use of the following documents in the selection process:
   - Reference
   - Person specification.

Intermediate 2

1. Define the term 'short-listing'.

2. Describe the purpose of a reference.

3. Suggest a disadvantage of a CV.

4. Suggest two advantages of an interview.

5. Suggest two disadvantages of an interview.

6. Describe the purpose of an assessment centre.

Training and development

Types of training

Businesses provide training to help employees carry out their jobs. The different types of training are:

Induction training

Induction training provides new employees with an introduction to the business. It usually takes place as soon as employees begin their new jobs.

Topics covered include an introduction to the business, health and safety procedures, location of toilets/canteen facilities and an introduction to the tasks involved in the job.

Top Tip
You should be able to **describe** different types of training and give advantages and disadvantages.

Advantages of induction training
• It allows the new employee to settle into their new working environment and job as quickly as possible.
• Important matters, such as health and safety training, can be carried out immediately.

On-the-job training

This is where training takes place within the business the employee works for.

Advantages	Disadvantages
• Less expensive than off-the-job training. • Helps to create good working relationships within the business.	• Training might be given by someone who has bad work habits. • Work is still expected to be carried out.

Off-the-job training

This is where training takes place outwith the business the employee works for. The training might be provided by, for example, a college or a specialist training company.

Advantages	Disadvantages
• Employee may gain a recognised qualification. • High-quality training is provided by experienced trainers.	• There is no output while employees are away being trained. • The cost of travelling to the training provider could be high if they are far away from the location of the business.

Appraisals

An appraisal is a meeting between an employee and employer that takes place on a yearly basis. It is an opportunity to find out what is going well for the employee and what is not going so well. Opportunities for the employee to receive training may be identified and targets for improvement might be set.

Appraisal systems

An **appraisal system** aims to ensure employees are working to the highest possible standards, with the goal of achieving the business's aims. An appraisal system allows the employees' strengths and development needs to be identified. Normally employees would meet annually with their line managers to discuss:

- what they are doing well
- what they feel is not going so well
- what could be done better
- what action could be taken to improve (for example, by setting targets).

A written record of the appraisal meeting will be kept and where an employee has development needs, he or she would normally be given the opportunity to undertake appropriate training to improve.

Benefits of appraisal systems	Costs of appraisal systems
• Those who have the potential to be promoted can be identified. • Employees receive feedback from their line managers. • Employees can become motivated if appraisals have been positive. • Opportunities for employees to develop skills and performance are identified.	• Employees can become demotivated if appraisals have not been positive. • It is time-consuming for organisations to carry out. • Too many development needs could be identified, resulting in stress for employees and increases in workload.

An **informal appraisal system** can also exist whereby no formal structure is followed. It could simply take the form of a chat at which the employee receives praise for doing a task well or is given feedback on how to improve their performance next time.

Top Tip
Both formal and informal appraisal systems exist.

Costs and benefits of training

We have already identified some of the advantages and disadvantages of different types of training. In the table below, some of these advantages and disadvantages have been explained. What you need to add to your answer to explain it is highlighted in red.

Benefits explained	Costs explained
• Employees can become more motivated and therefore more productive. • Quantity of wastage is lowered and costs are reduced. • The quality of the work the employee is carrying out will improve and the customer will get a better product or service and will be more likely to make a repeat purchase. • It contributes towards giving the organisation a good reputation which may attract high quality employees in the future.	• Can be expensive for the business as working time is lost when employees are being trained. • Some employees may be reluctant or unwilling to receive training so it could be a waste of time and money for the business. • Once employees have been trained they may find a more highly paid job with a competitor and this means the business would lose skilled employees that they have invested money in.

Quick Test 38

Intermediate 1

1. Describe three types of training.

2. Define the term 'appraisal'.

Intermediate 2

1. Suggest two benefits of an appraisal system.

2. Explain two benefits of training.

3. Explain two costs of training.

Employee relations

Payment methods

Top Tip
Questions on payment methods are common.

Employees expect to be paid for the work that they carry out.

Different payment methods can be used depending on the business and the activities that it carries out.

Time rate	Employees are paid per hour worked. This way, they know exactly how much they will earn because their pay rates do not change.
Flat rate	Employees are paid a set amount per year which is divided into 12 equal monthly payments. This is also known as a salary.
Piece rate	Employees are paid per item produced in addition to a low flat rate. This can encourage employees to work harder so that they earn more money.
Overtime	After working a set amount of hours, overtime is paid for extra hours worked. Usually the amount paid per hour overtime is more than the normal hourly rate. It could be 'time and a half' or 'double time'.
Commission	The amount of commission an employee receives depends on the value of sales they have made. Commission is usually a % of the sales value the employee has made. It might be paid in addition to a flat rate amount or it might not.
Bonus	A bonus is an additional payment an employee might get, for instance, if he or she has exceeded productivity targets. It will be paid in addition to their flat rate.

Employee relations

Businesses have to try to maintain good relationships with their employees. The managers of a business have a particular responsibility in trying to do this. They can try to maintain good working relationships with employees by:

- having regular meetings between management and employees
- involving employees in decision-making
- having an appraisal system
- having an 'open door' policy
- having a works council.

Some employees might be chosen to create a **works council.** The works council is able to access information that relates to the business and can take part in decision-making that concerns employees. This helps to improve the relationship between employees and the business.

Industrial action

Employees who are unhappy with their working conditions or terms of employment have the option of undertaking **industrial action.** Industrial action has a negative impact on businesses and can take a variety of forms:

- **Strike** – employees refuse to enter the workplace.
- **Sit in** – employees refuse to work and simply *sit in* the workplace.
- **Work to rule** – only activities written in the job description are carried out.
- **Go slow** – employees deliberately work slower than normal.
- **Overtime ban** – employees refuse to work any extra time over the normal working hours.
- **Boycott** – a refusal to carry out a new duty or use a new piece of equipment.

Industrial action can have serious consequences for businesses:
- Production can stop as employees are no longer producing goods.
- Customers could be lost because their orders have not been met on time.
- A business's image and reputation could be damaged as a result of the negative publicity.

Contract of employment

A contract of employment is a formal written document given to an employee when he or she starts working for the business. It lays down the conditions on which the employee is being employed by the business, so that both employee and employer are clear about each other's responsibilities. It contains the following pieces of information:

Top Tip
You should be able to identify pieces of information contained in a contract of employment.

- job title
- the date employment began
- location of the job
- hours of work
- rate of pay
- holiday entitlement
- pension entitlement
- sickness benefits.

Quick Test 39

Intermediate 1

1. Define the term 'piece rate'.
2. Suggest an advantage of piece rate.
3. Define the term 'time rate'.
4. Suggest an advantage of time rate.

Intermediate 2

1. Identify four pieces of information contained in a contract of employment.
2. Describe three forms of industrial action.
3. Describe the purpose of a contract of employment.

Law and the workplace

Law in the workplace

The government has introduced laws that businesses must follow. These laws are designed to help protect employees at work. Some of these laws are:

- Equality Act 2010
- Health and Safety at Work Act 1974
- Equal Pay Act 1970
- Sex Discrimination Act 1975
- Race Relations Act 1976.

Employment law

Top Tip
You should be able to describe the purpose of different pieces of legislation.

Employment laws are designed to protect employees in the workplace.

Equal Pay Act 1970

This law aims to ensure that men and women are paid the same for doing jobs which are considered to be of the same value.

Employment Rights Act 1996

The legal rights and duties of both employer and employee are stated in this law. It states that:

- Employees have the right to be given written contract of employments within two months of starting jobs.
- Employees should be given payslips which detail how their pay has been calculated. (That is, payslips are itemised.)
- Employees have specific rights concerning termination of employment and maternity or paternity leave.

National Minimum Wage Regulations 1999

These regulations set out the minimum hourly rate that must be paid to employees. The rate payable depends on the age of the employee as follows: 16–17 year olds, 18–21 year olds and 22 years old or over.

Equal opportunity law

Equal opportunity laws are designed to ensure people of all backgrounds are treated fairly, not just in the workplace but also in their own personal lives.

Equality Act 2010

This Act aims to protect the individual rights of people and make existing equality legislation stronger and more up-to-date. It brings together other equal opportunity laws with the aim of ensuring everyone is treated fairly regardless of, for example, race, gender or sexual orientation.

Sex Discrimination Act 1975

This law aims to prevent the discrimination of people on the basis of their gender or marital status. It would be illegal, for example, for an organisation to provide different conditions of service for men and women.

Race Relations Act 1976

This law aims to prevent the discrimination of people on the basis of their race, colour, religion or ethnic origin.

Disability Discrimination Act 1995

This law aims to prevent discrimination of people on the basis of disability. Where necessary, organisations must make reasonable changes to allow those with disabilities to access workplaces.

Health and safety law

Health and Safety at Work Act 1974

This law states the responsibilities of both the employee and employer in ensuring health and safety in the workplace. It states that both have a responsibility to ensure health and safety. Employees must consider the health and safety of other people and not just of themselves.

ICT law

The Data Protection Act 1998

This Act sets out the way organisations collect, store, process and distribute information. It has eight principles:

1. Data should be obtained fairly and lawfully.
2. Data shall be used for the registered purpose only.
3. Data shall not be used or given to any other person without permission.
4. Data shall be relevant, adequate and not excessive for the purpose.
5. Data must be accurate and kept up-to-date.
6. Data shall not be kept for longer than is needed.
7. Data should be available to the person who it relates to and changed if it is not accurate.
8. Data should be secure. There must be steps taken to keep it safe from unauthorised access or from being lost.

The Computer Misuse Act 1990

The Computer Misuse Act is concerned with those people who intend to or have committed the offence of hacking into computer systems. The Act makes it illegal for people to:

- gain access to computer material without permission
- gain unauthorised access with intent to commit crime
- change computer material without permission.

Quick Test 40

Intermediate 1

1. Identify three pieces of employment legislation.
2. Name a piece of health and safety legislation.

Intermediate 2

1. Describe the purpose of the Equality Act 2010.
2. Describe the purpose of the Health and Safety at Work Act 1974.

Answers to Quick Tests

Quick Test 1
1. Needs are essential for us to be able to live whereas wants are extra things that we like to have.
2. Water, food, clothing, shelter.
3. Mobile phone, holiday, computer game, car, DVD/CD.
4. Dentist, hairdresser, hotel, bank, restaurant, transport providers (e.g. bus, train, air).
5. Adding value to materials by converting them from inputs to outputs.
6. Businesses that take raw materials from the ground or sea.
7. Supermarkets/shops, schools, hairdressers, dentists, airlines (any business that provides a service).

Quick Test 2
1. Land, labour, capital and enterprise.
2. The entrepreneur comes up with a business idea, makes decisions and is willing to take risks to make it successful. He or she will combine the four factors of production.
3. Richard Branson, Bill Gates, Anita Roddick, James Dyson.
4. The entrepreneur thinks of a business idea by looking at what already exists and then finding something new that people would want. He or she then brings together and combines different resources (factors of production: land, labour, capital and enterprise) to create a product. He or she has to make different decisions and take risks to turn the idea into a success.
5. Risk of losing their own financial investment, risk of people not wanting to buy the good/service that they have come up with.

1. Land – the natural resources of the world, such as fields, trees, water, sunshine. Labour – the human effort (the workforce) required to make a product. Capital – the machinery, tools and equipment used to make a product and the money (financial investment) used to start the business. Enterprise – combining all the factors of production, which is done by the entrepreneur.
2. Thinks of a new business idea by looking at what already exists so that he or she produces something that is more likely to be successful and profitable as it doesn't already exist. Brings together and combines the four factors of production in the most efficient and cost-effective way by ensuring that the best use of each one is being achieved. Makes different decisions (for example, what product to make, what price to charge and what staff to employ) with the intention of making the best decision in the best interests of the success of the business.

Quick Test 3
1. Private Limited Company.
2. Public Limited Company.
3. A business owned by one person.
4. Easy to set up; owner gets all the profits.
5. A business owned by 2–20 people.
6. More ideas available, responsibility/workload shared.
7. An organisation owned by the government and funded by taxes.
8. A charity.

Quick Test 4
1. To make a profit, to grow, to survive, to offer a quality good/service, to be market leader, to have a strong brand identity.
2. To provide a service, to meet the needs of local people, to stick to an agreed budget, to have a good image.
3. To help a particular cause, to spend donations in the best possible way, to increase the number of volunteers, to increase donations, to promote the cause/charity.
4. A target or goal to be worked towards.
5. To make a profit, to survive, to grow, to offer a quality product or service, to be the market leader, to have a strong brand identity.
6. To make a profit, to survive, to grow, to offer a quality product or service, to be the market leader, to have a strong brand identity.
7. To provide a service, to meet the needs of local people, to have a good image, to stick to an agreed budget.

8. To spend donations in the best possible way, to promote the charity/cause, to increase the number of volunteers, to increase donations.

1. To have more customers than any other business in the same market.
2. To only spend the amount of money that has been allocated.
3. To receive more money from members of the public to help the charity's cause through fundraising activities.

Quick Test 5
1. Owners (or shareholders), employees, managers.
2. Customers, suppliers, banks, government, local community.
3. They want good wages.
4. They want to pay a fair price.
5. They can take industrial action (e.g. a strike).
6. They can shop somewhere else.

1. They can take industrial action (e.g. a strike) which could result in lower productivity and lost orders.
2. They can increase the price they charge resulting in higher costs and lower profits for the business.
3. They can shop somewhere else resulting in lower profits for the business.

Quick Test 6
1. Bank loan, loan from family/friends, government grant, issuing shares.
2. Loan of money from a bank repaid over time with interest.
3. Usually easy and quick to get.
4. Money from the government that usually has conditions attached to it.
5. Does not have to be paid back.

1. Bank overdraft, hire purchase.
2. Usually easy and quick to get which means money can be accessed if needed quickly or in an emergency.
3. Interest has to be paid which makes the loan more expensive and therefore more is repaid than has been received.

Quick Test 7
1. Poor management, poorly trained staff, little/no finance, poor stock control.
2. Introduction of new laws, change in the interest rate, increased competition, fall in demand, change in the weather.
3. Business might be poorly controlled and wrong decisions might be made.
4. Payments on loans, could be higher or lower depending on whether the rate goes up or down.

1. PESTEC.
2. Fall in demand, changes in interest rates.
3. Changes in fashion/trends, changes in working practices.
4. The business might have to provide more training to staff which could be expensive.
5. This could cause a business to lose customers if it does not lower its price or provide a better quality product than its competitors.

Quick Test 8
1. To increase sales, to increase profit, to reduce risk, to increase market share.
2. A multinational organisation is one that operates in more than one country.
3. The benefits a business gets from being big.

1. One large business takes ownership and control of another smaller one.
2. Two businesses of the same size agree to become one.
3. Backward vertical integration means taking over a supplier whereas forward vertical integration means taking over a customer.
4. A franchise is where someone starts a business and provides a product or service supplied by another business (including using the name and brand of the other business).

Quick Test 9

1. The source of information is where the information comes from, whereas the type of information is the way the information is presented and what it looks like.
2. Staff records, sales figures, final accounts, minutes from meetings.
3. Bar graph, line graph, pie chart.
4. This is information gathered from the organisation's own records.
5. Information presented through photographs or pictures.
6. Information that is spoken and heard by someone else.
7. Information presented through a graph or chart.

1. The source of the information is known so it is more reliable than secondary information.
2. Easy to obtain and usually cheap saving the organisation money/time on carrying out research which would impact upon profitability.
3. Unique to the organisation and so more relevant to the decision being made or the task in hand.
4. Source of the information might not be known and the information could therefore be unreliable.
5. Can be kept as a record for later reference and does not rely on memory to recall important facts.
6. An instant response is given which means questions can be asked and information or decisions communicated immediately.
7. Can make comparisons easily and decisions based on this can be made more easily.
8. Quantitative information is factual information that can be measured or counted whereas qualitative information is information in the form of opinions or views.

Quick Test 10

1. To make decisions, to monitor costs, to check employee work rates, to monitor how well the business is doing, to identify new business opportunities, to check how much profit is being made.
2. Owners, management, creditors, employees, competitors, customers, citizens.
3. To check the performance of the business and how successful decision-making has been.
4. To check if the business is making a profit so that they can argue for a pay rise or better working conditions.
5. To check if the business will be creating new jobs in the future.

1. Information is used to inform new plans or to make predictions and decisions about what may happen in the future.
2. Information is used to check how well the business is doing. Once this has been done, it may involve making decisions to improve performance.
3. Using information to see where there are opportunities to meet the needs and wants of more customers by coming up with a new business idea and then developing it.

Quick Test 11

1. To help with decision-making; to collect, store and distribute information; to communicate with customers and other stakeholders; to maintain records.
2. Monitor, mouse, keyboard, printer, scanner, speakers, modem.
3. It displays information from the computer on a screen.
4. To create an electronic copy of a paper document.
5. Spreadsheet software allows numerical information to be stored, calculated recalled and edited.
6. A password is a unique piece of information that only the user of a computer should know. It is used to gain access to a computer system.
7. A copy of all the information, files and programs on the system and keeping it secure just in case something happens to the original version.

Quick Test 12

1. Computer, modem, telephone line and internet browsing software.
2. Uniform Resource Locator. This is the website address that needs to be typed in to access a website.
3. Product information (e.g. price, pictures), opening hours, address/directions to business.

4. To reach customers worldwide at any time of day; to cut down on costs (such as rent on a shop); to collect information about customers; to advertise and promote their business.
5. Email is used to send an electronic message to another person via their email address.
6. Where a computer link is set up between people in different locations to allow them to see and hear each other.
7. Staff require training, cost of purchasing hardware/software, viruses.

Quick Test 13

1. To enter, edit and delete appointments.
2. Appointment reminders can be set, regularly-occurring appointments can be entered, other people's diaries can be searched quickly.
3. Local Area Network.
4. A group of computers linked together. These computers could be in different locations.
5. To make telephone calls, to send text messages, to take photographs, to access the internet, to play games.

1. Data and information can be processed much more quickly than by traditional methods; improved decision-making is possible as more information can be accessed; employee wage costs may be reduced if technology replaces the need for them; communication between departments, branches and customers can improve through, for example, email; better work rates and higher productivity can be achieved.
2. It can be expensive to install and maintain hardware/software; employees require training in using technology; employees may be reluctant to use new technologies; employees may feel unvalued and less motivated if they feel technology is replacing their jobs or parts of their jobs; technology can break down and have faults, which is costly not only in terms of getting it fixed, but also time and, if production stops, the organisation's output also stops.

Quick Test 14

1. Planning, organising, commanding, co-ordinating and controlling.
2. Long-term decisions concerned with the overall direction, purpose and focus of the organisation.
3. To expand into a foreign country, to diversify into new products, to maximise sales.
4. Medium-term decisions concerned with actions to achieve strategic decisions.
5. Find cheaper suppliers of raw materials in order to cut costs, expand range of goods or services offered to grow customer base.
6. Short-term decisions which affect the day-to-day running of the organisation.
7. Train staff in the new products available, decisions on staff working hours for next week.
8. Planning, organising, controlling, coordination, communication, leadership, patience.

Quick Test 15

1. POGADSCIE.
2. Nine.
3. Identify the problem, identify the objectives, gather information, analyse the gathered information, devise possible solutions, select the best solution, communicate the decision, implement the decision, evaluate the decision.
4. Time is given to think about and consider the range of options (alternatives) available; different factors that may impact upon the decision can be considered provided time permits; the effectiveness and impact of each decision is considered during the evaluation stage; no quick decisions are made because time is given to gather information.
5. It takes time to gather information and it might be difficult to obtain good quality information; the impact of each solution cannot be fully seen when options are being considered; it may be difficult to think of different solutions to complicated or unusual problems; instinct and gut reactions of managers to situations are stifled because they are following a sequential process.

Quick Test 16
1. Marketing, Finance, Operations, Human Resources, Research & Development.
2. A group of people coming together for a common purpose, goal or aim.
3. To show how an organisation is internally structured and how departments interact.
4. Grouping by functional areas (departments), e.g. Human Resources, Operations, Marketing, Finance and perhaps Research and Development. People working in these departments will carry out similar tasks.
5. A tall structure has many layers whereas a flat structure has few.
6. The number of subordinates (people) who report to a person.
7. Being answerable for decisions and actions taken.
8. Having the power to make decisions and to take particular actions.
9. Giving the authority and responsibility to carry out a particular task or action to someone else.
10. This shows how instructions are passed down through an organisation.

Quick Test 17
1. Informal communication that is not shown in the formal organisation structure.
2. A relationship between people on the same level of the organisation structure.
3. One department providing a service to another.
4. Activities being carried out by another organisation.
5. Downsizing.

Quick Test 18
1. Finding out what customers want, advertising products, researching what competitors are doing and deciding on the prices of products.
2. Product, price, place, promotion.
3. To attract new customers, to increase profit levels, to enter new markets, to help the business grow, to help the business survive.
4. This is how the customer is made aware of the product and the ways they are encouraged to buy it. (It's more than just advertising!)
5. This is how much a business charges for its product.
6. Customers need to be aware that a product exists and why they should buy it or they will not purchase it.
7. Customers will not buy a product if it costs too much because they might be able to buy it cheaper elsewhere.

1. The proportion of customers that a business has in a market.
2. The business that has the most customers in a market.
3. Market research has identified the need for a product and the business produces it to satisfy the needs of its customers.
4. A product is produced because the business thinks it is the best at producing it and/or it faces little or no competition.

Quick Test 19
1. Introduction, growth, maturity and decline.
2. The product life cycle shows the stages of the product's life.
3. This is the good or service being sold by the business.
4. Businesses must supply customers with the product they want or the business will not make any sales or profit.

1. Development, introduction, growth, maturity, saturation, decline.
2. Development – the product is developed by the business. Introduction – the product is introduced to/launched onto the market. Growth – sales of the product grow quickly. Maturity – product sales at the highest point. Saturation – product sales begin to decrease as product has saturated the market. Decline – sales of the product are decreasing.
3. A method of injecting new life into a product to keep it selling.
4. Change the appearance of the packaging as this gives the product a new image and will appeal to customers. Change the product, for example, its size, variety or shape, as this makes the product different from the original version and the customer will feel they are getting something newer. Improve the quality of the product, for example, by using

higher quality raw materials, as this will improve the way the product is seen by customers, giving it a better image. Change the way the product is promoted, for example, offer a 20% discount, as this will encourage customers to buy it as they are getting it cheaper. Increase advertising of the product, for example, by advertising it on TV, as this will increase awareness of the product and what it can do.

Quick Test 20
1. Gender, income, occupation, age, social class or religious belief.
2. The name, symbol or logo given to a group or type of product.
3. Repeat purchases, higher profit, easier to introduce new products under the brand.
4. The group of people or type of person a business focuses its product towards.

1. Specific market segments can have products tailored to requirements; prices can be set to reflect the market segment, for example, higher prices could be charged; prevents money being wasted on promoting products to the wrong market segment; products can be sold in the most appropriate place for the market segment and where these customers are most able to access them.
2. Brand loyalty can be established with customers which will lead to repeat purchases; branded products are often associated with quality and the customer may be more likely to purchase them because of this; higher prices can often be charged and this results in higher profits; brands are easily and quickly recognised by customers helping to distinguish them from competitors' products; new products with the brand name can be introduced successfully as the name is already well-known.
3. Poor brands can have serious consequences for the business as customers may associate the whole product range with poor quality and not buy any of the products; brands can be copied or fakes produced and sold to try to give the impression they are the real item; it is time consuming and expensive for a business to establish a brand and this will impact upon the business's profitability.

Quick Test 21
1. Low price, high price, penetration pricing, price skimming, destroyer pricing.
2. This is the amount charged for the product.
3. Customers will shop elsewhere if the price is too high.
4. The price charged is lower than that of competitors.
5. The price charged is higher than that of competitors.

1. Customers will buy the product as the price is lower than competitors' prices.
2. It forces competition out of the market.
3. For new and exclusive products.
4. The product's life cycle position; how much competitors charge for their product; the cost of making the product or providing the service; the level of profit that is wanted; the market segment that the product is focused towards; how much of the product can be supplied.

Quick Test 22
1. Shops/supermarkets, online, through TV shopping channels, over the telephone and through the post.
2. The way the business gets the product to the customer and where the product is sold.
3. Customers need to be able to access the product in the most convenient place.

1. Manufacturer → Customer,
   Manufacturer → Retailer → Customer,
   Manufacturer → Wholesaler → Customer,
   Manufacturer → Wholesaler → Retailer → Customer.
2. The route the product takes to get from the manufacturer to the customer.
3. A wholesaler buys large quantities of items from the manufacturer and then sells them on to retailers.
4. A business which distributes products to the customer on behalf of the manufacturer.
5. The actual product and its life cycle; the image the manufacturer wants the product to have; availability of finance; reputation and reliability of wholesalers and retailers.

Quick Test 23

1. Advertising, special offers, free samples, celebrity endorsement.
2. Promotion is how the customer is made aware that the product exists.
3. If people didn't know the product existed, they couldn't buy it.
4. Informing people that a product exists and giving them information about it.
5. Providing the customer with a discount, such as 25% off or BOGOF.

1. Customers worldwide can be targeted; customers can buy online 24/7 from a place of their choice; online discounts are often given; product information can be updated and accessed quickly; stock availability can be checked and items reserved before purchasing.
2. Customer is unable to handle or see the goods fully; customers may be unwilling to leave their personal or credit/debit card details; there may be computer or internet problems while ordering; the customer has no personal contact with the organisation.
3. Using a celebrity to promote a business's product(s)

Quick Test 24

1. Researching the market to find out what customers want.
2. Gathering new information from the market.
3. Using old information that already exists.
4. Surveys, interviews, observations.
5. Books, magazines, internet websites.
6. To gather both verbal and non-verbal (e.g. body language) information.
7. To obtain answers to specific questions about a product.

1. Desk research involves looking at existing information whereas field research involves gathering new information.
2. Postal survey – this is when people are sent a questionnaire through the post. Telephone survey – this is when people are contacted by telephone and asked to answer a series of questions. Personal interview – this involves a face-to-face, two-way process whereby a researcher (the interviewer) asks a person a number of questions and they will respond orally with their answer. Focus group – a discussion between a selected number of people and an experienced researcher. Hall test – this involves a product being given to customers to try and then obtaining their opinions and views. Observation – this involves watching something and recording what happens.
3. Easy to obtain and usually cheap, saving the organisation money/time on carrying out field research which would impact upon profitability; quick to find information on the internet and decisions can therefore be made quickly.
4. The information gathered is first hand (is new) and is more reliable than existing information; information is gathered for a specific purpose so is more relevant and purposeful to the decision being made.
5. Random sampling – randomly selecting people from a list. Stratified random sampling – sampling on a certain group of people, based on how the population as a whole is divided. Quota sampling – selecting a number of people to question based on certain characteristics.
6. People's feelings and views can be obtained.
7. Relatively inexpensive to carry out; customers get to try the product for themselves and can report back on it.

Quick Test 25

1. Operations manufactures products; turns inputs into outputs.
2. Turning inputs into outputs; meeting customer demand by making products they want; using production resources in the best way possible; managing stock levels; choosing a suitable supplier of raw materials.
3. The ingredients (the basic items) that are used to manufacture a product.
4. The cost of the raw materials, the quality of the raw materials, the time that it will take for raw materials to be delivered, the quantity that can be delivered, the storage space available, how reliable the supplier is.

1. System design, system operation, purchasing.
2. System design – this element is concerned with deciding the best way to organise work (i.e. the flow or process of production). It considers the best way products should be made and the best way to distribute products once they have been made. System operation – ensuring there are enough raw materials to keep production going. It involves making sure that there is the correct quantity of raw materials available when needed in the manufacturing process. Purchasing – buying the raw materials from a supplier to be used in the production process.

Quick Test 26

1. Raw materials, goods currently being made, finished goods.
2. Production could stop as there are not enough materials; customers might not receive their orders on time; could give a poor image which could result in losing customers.
3. Could be costly (for example, paying for storage); stock is at higher risk of being stolen; stock might become out of date.
4. A method of recording stock levels manually.

1. Centralised stock storage means all stock is held in one place whereas decentralised stock storage means stock is held in more than one place.
2. Stock is delivered just in time for it to be used in the production process.
3. Money is not tied up in stock; saves money in paying for storage costs; less chance of stock being stolen; less chance of stock going to waste, e.g. through deterioration.
4. The system automatically reorders stock when it is required; can tell quickly which products are selling well and which ones are not (useful to management in making decisions); a count of stock by hand is no longer required.
5. The system could be expensive to purchase; staff require training in using the system; upgrades to the system might be necessary and could be expensive.

Quick Test 27

1. Machinery, rather than people, is used to make something.
2. A mixture of people and machinery is used to make a product.
3. Unique/one-off products are made to the customer's specification, e.g. handmade chocolates, piece of art, a wedding cake.
4. Identical products are produced in batches and move to the next stage of production together, e.g. newspapers, cakes, bread.
5. Each item moves along a production line where another part is added, e.g. electrical items, cars, computers.

1. The exact demands of the customer can be met resulting in a better service being offered and a happier customer; high prices can be charged as customers are often willing to pay higher prices for exclusive or unique products; the design can be changed to suit the individual customer requirement even when production has begun and this gives the customer a sense of ownership over what is being made.
2. Batches can be changed to suit the requirements and demands of the customer resulting in a better service being offered and a happier customer; cost savings can be made compared to job production which means the product will be more profitable.
3. Large quantities of identical products can be made compared to job production where it could take a long time to produce only one; machinery is often used for the whole production process and therefore no employees need to be paid; raw materials can be purchased in bulk, saving the business money; machinery can work 24 hours a day, 7 days a week whereas people cannot as they require breaks and rest.
4. Labour intensive production is where people are used to make products whereas capital intensive production is where machinery is used to make products.

Quick Test 28

1. So that customers purchase the product.
2. They can use high quality raw materials; they can train their staff to a high standard; they can use a good quality supplier; they can update and maintain the machinery used in production; they can use quality assurance.

3. Checking products at various stages during production.
4. BS Kite Mark.

1. Customers may make repeat purchases in the future; a good reputation can be established which encourages new customers; customers will not purchase from a competitor; profit can be maximised; the business can grow and increase its market share; wastage will be minimised and the cost of production kept low.
2. Checking the product once it has been manufactured.
3. Comparing one product with another similar product, often using the market leader's standards as the benchmark
4. Members of the organisation meeting regularly with management to discuss quality issues and to attempt to find ways to solve these.
5. Recruit and select appropriately skilled and qualified individuals; provide high quality training; have a system in place for recognising employees' strengths and areas for improvement,

Quick Test 29
1. Paying bills, maintaining financial records, paying wages and salaries.
2. To manage the business's money (financial resources).

1. To enable costs and expenditure to be controlled; to enable cash flow going in and out of the business to be monitored; to forecast what might happen in the future; to monitor performance; to provide management with information for decision-making.
2. Maintaining financial records – records of the money coming into and going out of the business – have to be kept. Paying bills – suppliers have to be paid on time and other bills, such as electricity, also have to be paid. Paying wages and salaries – employees have to be paid for the work that they carry out.
3. To ensure the business maintains a good reputation and good relationships with its suppliers and to enable it to maintain a good credit rating.
4. They could become unhappy, demotivated and take industrial action.

Quick Test 30
1. This shows a summary of the money that has come in and gone out of the business over a particular period of time (usually one year) and the profit that has been made.
2. This shows the worth/value of the business.
3. Profit made from buying and selling goods before expenses are subtracted.
4. Amount of profit made after expenses have been subtracted from the gross profit.
5. Money the owner has taken out of the business for their own personal use.
6. Items that the business owns that will last longer than one year.
7. Vehicles, premises, land, machinery.
8. Items that the business owns that will last for less than one year.
9. Stock, cash, debtors.
10. Short-term (under one year) debts.
11. Creditors.
12. People the business owes money to.
13. People who owe money to the business.

Quick Test 31
1. Seeking cheaper suppliers of raw materials; selling assets no longer needed; increasing advertising and marketing activities; increasing or decreasing the price of a product.
2. Finding cheaper suppliers of raw materials; cutting overtime paid to employees; seeking cheaper sources of electricity.
3. The cash budget shows the expected receipts (inflows) and payments (outflows) of cash over a period of time.

1. Introducing JIT; offering cash discounts to customers who pay on time; increase advertising/promotion; selling assets no longer required; taking out a bank loan; checking the reliability of customers; increasing capital from shareholders/owners.

2. Having money tied up in stock; too much time given to customers to pay debts (long credit periods); not enough money being made from sales; too short a credit period being offered by creditors or suppliers; high value of drawings taken out by owners; spending money on fixed assets and other capital items (such as machines).
3. Stock is only purchased when it is required (hence 'just in time') to meet a customer order and therefore saves cash being tied up in unused/unnecessary stock.

Quick Test 32
1. Management, employees, trade unions, shareholders, creditors/lenders, suppliers, local community, government.
2. To see if decisions they have made have been effective; to enable planning for the future so that the business can achieve its objectives (such as growth).
3. To see whether or not the business is paying a fair wage based on the profit it is making – it might be possible to negotiate a higher pay claim; if profit is good, better working conditions and other benefits could be argued for.
4. To see if the business is making profit and will survive in order to provide and protect jobs in the local area.
5. Financial information is historical and does not take into account what might happen in the future or the result of any recent change.

Quick Test 33
1. Gross Profit Percentage, Net Profit Percentage, Current Ratio, Mark Up Ratio, Acid Test Ratio, Return on Capital Employed
2. This ratio shows the profit made from the buying and selling of stock.

$$\frac{\text{Gross Profit}}{\text{Sales}} \times 100 = \underline{} \%$$

3. This ratio shows the profit made once expenses have been paid by the organisation.

$$\frac{\text{Net Profit}}{\text{Sales}} \times 100 = \underline{} \%$$

4. This ratio shows how able an organisation is to pay off its short-term debts.

$$\frac{\text{Current Assets}}{\text{Current Liabilities}} : 1$$

5. Selling price was raised, cheaper suppliers were used, higher sales due to better marketing.
6. Gross profit was higher, expenses have been cheaper (e.g. cheaper electricity).

Quick Test 34
1. Human Resource Management.
2. Recruiting and selecting new staff, staff training, carrying out appraisals, providing safe working conditions, complying with employment laws, dealing with employee discipline and grievances.
3. To deal with and manage employee-related issues.

1. Employees are given flexibility in their starting and finishing times. They usually have to be present during 'core time' which would be set by the business.
2. People can balance their personal and work commitments more easily and therefore have a better work/life balance; own start and finish times can often be chosen; travelling time and cost can be reduced; less stressful as they are more in control of their work and personal commitments.
3. Staff are generally more motivated and are therefore more productive; there will be a reduced number of absences and incidents of late starting; space and money can be saved in the office if employees are working out of the office; potential employees may be attracted to a business which offers flexible working practices.
4. Homeworking involves people working from home whereas teleworking involves working outwith the office on the go. Both types of workers use ICT to communicate with the organisation.
5. How hard a person is willing to work.